Culture of Opportunity

How to Grow Your Business
In An Age of Disruption

By Mark Monchek

Founder and Chief Opportunity Officer of The Opportunity Lab

"We need to act our way to a new way of thinking."

June Holley, Author, The Network Weaver

Published by The Opportunity Lab Press.
2017
Copyright © 2016 by THE OPPORTUNITY LAB
ISBN-13: 978-0-692-81125-2

Printed by Lulu.com
Book Design by Pollen Brands, pollenbrands.com
Cover Design by Ivan Popov, ivan@avgd.rs

www.opplab.com
Email: discover@opplab.com

In Dedication

To my parents, Barbara Shilo and Meyer Monchek, and the generations who came before them.

It is my deepest wish that this book honors their life's work in making a better world.

Table of Contents

The arrogance of success is thinking that what you did yesterday will be sufficient for tomorrow.

William Pollard, Quaker Minister and Co-Author of A Reasonable Faith

Turn Disruption into Opportunity

We all know it: today, radical disruption is nothing unusual. In fact, disruption has become the norm. Every day, life-changing events — like terrorist attacks, weather catastrophes, disease outbreaks, the rise of fringe political candidates, and mass migration due to war — overturn the existing reality.

Yet, as the world changes radically and continuously, the way many of us run our organizations sadly stays the same.

The leaders of many organizations still act as if their world is relatively stable and predictable, and the business practices they follow stem from this flawed belief. For instance, these leaders think the future can be predicted through standard market research, drawn from the opinions of a relatively small number of customers and an analysis of what competitors are offering now, rather than what they will offer. They also think that the future can be planned for by a small group of senior executives, as if this group has an expansive enough view of the world with all its complications.

Business practices such as these are obsolete, only many leaders don't realize it.

This is a time of radical transition. Some of what we're headed for is harmful, but much of it can be good. We're leaving behind an era where exploited labor produced wealth by extracting finite material resources like gold, oil, and steel, and we've started an era where wealth is created through the creative interplay of ideas and technology. We're moving from a reliance on scarce reserves and cultures of competition to a focus on abundant, renewable resources and collaboration.

> The best way to thrive in such a new world is by becoming an expert. What type? An expert in opportunity.

The best way to thrive in such a new world is by becoming an expert. What type? An expert in opportunity. When you're an expert in opportunity you can see opportunity even in the most unusual places. You understand which opportunities are right for your company and engage the right key people in the process of making decisions and executing effectively.

Becoming an Opportunity Expert

How, then, do you become an opportunity expert? I see three keys.

Opportunity Expert Key 1: Mindset

You must develop an opportunity mindset. That is, when unexpected challenges emerge, even when those challenges seem insurmountable, you must instinctively ask, "What is the opportunity here?" I don't mean being naïve and underestimating the problem. I mean looking at those situations with a clear eye, and objectively looking to develop solutions that are realistic and fit your organization's values, competencies, and resources.

Opportunity Expert Key 2: Nature

You must work with, rather than against, the natural order of things. This means both the natural world as well as the nature of people and organizations. This starts with fully acknowledging the sacredness of life. For decades, America's form of capitalism ignored the cost of trying to subdue nature, including human nature. Now, with greater awareness of what needs to be done to reverse this damage, a new generation of entrepreneurs are harnessing the power of nature through innovative uses of wind power, solar energy and biomimicry. They are employing the power of human nature by creating organizations that are run more by collaboration and consensus rather than by command and control.

Opportunity Expert Key 3: Culture

Your entire organizational culture must revolve around opportunity. This means that the culture supports and nurtures contributions from every corner of the organization. From the crew who cleans the stores at night, to the customer service agents who field complaints, to data scientists who gather and analyze information, and so on. No ideas are shunned; taking risks and sometimes failing is encouraged.

How This Book Is Organized

Before we begin, let me briefly tell you how this book is laid out, and what you'll come away with after reading it. I've divided the material into six sections.

In Part One

The Need for a *Culture of Opportunity*, I'll talk briefly about the American Dream: what its promise was, how that promise was subverted, and how a vibrant opportunity focus can reinvigorate the Dream.

In Part Two

How to Build an Opportunity Driven Business That Will Thrive in Any Economy, I'll introduce you to the methodology that will enable you to create a culture that can spot, generate, and evaluate opportunity. You'll learn about the opportunity mindset and how to build your own *opportunity team*. Included in this section is my firm's seven-step "how-to" formula for creating such a spirited game-changing team and how it can help you find success.

In Part Three

the *Culture of Opportunity* in Action, I'll present you with three Opportunity Stories. These are case studies showing the methodology in action, demonstrating the impactful results our clients achieved from the process, along with a handful of lessons learned. Once you understand how the cultural aspects of opportunity-building work, the next two sections describe important personal refinements that might be particularly useful to you as a leader.

In Part Four

Principles of a Conscious Leader, I'll discuss three key approaches that will help you, as a leader, be more in tune with your organization, society, and the world. This section, in essence, will help you be more conscious of your role as a steward.

In Part Five

Conclusion: The Challenge of Scale, I will review the key concepts you've learned and the Action Steps you can take to build a *Culture of Opportunity* at your organization. I will show you how you can overcome the challenge of reaching the appropriate scale for your company.

In Part Six

The *Culture of Opportunity* Toolkit, I'll provide you with a series of assessments, exercises and resources that you can use to enhance your abilities as an opportunity master. At the conclusion, you'll walk away with your own *Opportunity Plan*, which you can use to turn your vision into an appropriate opportunity.

OK, *let's begin.*

Discovering the Culture of Opportunity Process

How did I start my company, The *Opportunity Lab*, with its focus on opportunity and develop the *Culture of Opportunity* process? It didn't begin as part of a boardroom strategy session. Instead, it grew out of the pain of extreme adversity.

In 2007, I was running a company called PerformXcellence, which helped companies develop strategic plans for long term growth and support their execution of those plans. We were having our best year... or so I thought.

I will never forget the moment that changed my life. One morning, as I arrived at Kennedy airport in a taxi on the way to Atlanta, my credit card was declined. That didn't make sense. I had more than enough credit. A week later, I was at a restaurant paying for dinner when a different card was rejected. How was that possible? Soon checks were bouncing and purchases had to be cancelled. A short while later I discovered why. It was all terribly disorienting.

In the midst of our record sales year, a highly-placed employee had been committing fraud – on a grand scale. Rather than record profits in the bank, my company was running on fumes.

Of course I was the CEO, but I hadn't involved myself in all parts of the business as I should have. I spent most of my time doing the things I enjoyed and was good at: like winning new clients and delivering the work product. I figured that I'm the one who brought in the money, let someone else take care of the bookkeeping. I told myself I was too busy to do any monitoring. Naturally, my logic was flawed, and I paid the price.

I had not only let my company and my employees down, I felt I had let my family down even more. I could barely sleep at night. It was just as hard waking up each morning. I became more and more morose, and my thoughts grew darker. Meanwhile, the state of the economy was tumbling just as fast. My own situation, coupled with the frightening state of the economy, became too much for me. Eventually, I checked into a hospital.

> It felt like waking up from a nightmare and finding out that not only was my life not over, but a richer and more purposeful life had just begun.

What was the strange thing about this? Years earlier, when I was in graduate school, I worked on an inpatient psychiatric unit. Now, I was experiencing being on the other side of the bed. I paced the halls and asked myself how I could have possibly given up on life. But as bad as my situation had become, a new thought began bubbling up inside of me which would end up changing everything. As I walked up and down those grim halls, I asked myself: "How can I take my life back?"

Soon, because of that question, a shift started taking place inside of me. At first, it was slight, but soon it picked up momentum. By the time I had left the hospital, this new feeling began to overwhelm me. What was it I was experiencing?

Gratitude.

I had always considered myself a grateful person, but having almost ruined my life infused me with an experience of gratitude that was now at the very core of my being. It felt like waking up from a nightmare and finding out that not only was my life not over, but a richer and more purposeful life had just begun.

> Everywhere I looked I saw a word that symbolized everything this new life had to offer. That word: Opportunity.

Suddenly, like a guardian angel whispering in my ear, everywhere I looked I saw a word that symbolized everything this new life had to offer. That word: Opportunity.

Back at work, I began seeing the difference between the companies that were managing their way through the broken economy (many later to grow stronger as a result) and those that were stricken by fear and confusion.

We began encouraging our clients to ask, "What is the opportunity in this economy? What is there in this crisis that could make you a stronger company?"

Over the next two years, I studied our clients that were successfully managing through the 2008 recession and compared them to those that were not. I looked at the extraordinary companies that had become iconic brands and that had grown stronger during the crisis. Google, Apple, Netflix, Uber, AirBnB, Comcast, Bristol-Myers Squibb, JP Morgan Chase, TED, Zappos, Amazon, Starbucks, Costco, and Facebook were among them.

In 2010, I renamed our company The *Opportunity Lab*, and began putting more fully into practice what I had learned. As I gained some distance from the trauma, I began to ask myself "What would have happened if the theft had never occurred?" I had thought of this incident as a tragedy of unfathomable magnitude and me as victim, worthy of great sympathy.

But, now that I was reinventing our business, having more fun, feeling more blessed than ever, and experiencing some breakthrough results with clients..."I wondered, how could this have happened if the 'tragedy' never happened?" This was another lesson to me that opportunity may be found at the most inopportune times.

The more I reflected on what we had been doing before the crash, I realized that it was in some ways a much better version of what we had been doing before. It was a very different version of what had come before.

> We created a step-by-step method for our clients to create a Culture of Opportunity.

The *Opportunity Lab* was still helping companies develop and execute a plan for growth. The big difference was that rather than focusing on trying to help our clients predict the future through a long term plan, we created a step-by-step method for our clients to create a *Culture of Opportunity*.

A culture that is structured yet also understands that the radically different world of business demands a radically different way of operating.

With extreme wealth comes extreme responsibility. And the responsibility for me comes with creating new businesses, create jobs, employ people and put money aside to tackle issues where we can make a difference.

Richard Branson, Entrepreneur, Author and Philanthropist

PART ONE

The Need for a
Culture of Opportunity

The Evolution of the American
Dream and American Business

Since its inception, America has been known as the land of opportunity. Throughout its history, hundreds of millions of people from around the world have come here to pursue the American Dream. They've sought the opportunity to live in a safe home and in a community of their choice to enable them to do meaningful work in a well-paying job with access to education and healthcare. What's more, they've looked for ways to make continual progress — both for themselves and their family.

Several generations of my ancestors — along with two million Jews from Eastern Europe between 1880 and 1920 — came to the United States with little more than a steamer trunk and a dream. Vast numbers of them rose into the middle class and beyond... in one generation. Each successive generation was expected to prosper and achieve greater access to what America offered. Yet, over the past four decades, the dream has faded.

I come from a long line of entrepreneurs. Shown above are the founders of Shepher Distributors & Sales Company. My five uncles (George, Bill, Irving, Danny and Eddie Monchik) and aunt, (Lillian Polner) are pictured with my parents, (Meyer and Barbara) and other relatives, circa 1945.

> For many, The American Dream has become a nightmare of debt, unemployment, unaffordable or substandard education, spotty healthcare and shoddy housing.

Today, fewer Americans are improving their station. For many, The American Dream has become a nightmare of debt, unemployment, unaffordable or substandard education, spotty healthcare and shoddy housing.

When I was growing up in the 1950s and 1960s, one person's wages – made while working as, say, a bus driver, nurse, school teacher or factory worker -- was enough to buy a home and a car while raising a family. Writes Robert Reich in his book Saving Capitalism:

"For three decades after World War II, America created the largest middle class the world has ever seen. During those years, the earnings of a typical American worker doubled just as the size of the American economy doubled. Over the next thirty years, by contrast, the size of the economy doubled again, but the earnings of the typical worker went nowhere. Then the CEO of a large corporation earned an average of about twenty times the pay of the typical worker. Now, they get over two hundred times. In those years, the richest segment of Americans took home 9 to 10 percent of total income, today the top 1 percent gets 20 percent." (Reich, 2015)

During the post-war boom years (and, in fact, long before that), the American Dream had become a reality for a large segment of Americans.

Today, however, more people are worried about their future than at any time since the Great Depression. In a 2015 report from the US Government Accountability Office, 40.4 percent of Americans worked at contingent jobs in 2010, up from 35.3 percent in 2006 (Jeszeck, 2015).

According to the Bureau of Labor Statistics, 7.2 million Americans work multiple part-time jobs, representing 4.9% of all workers (Labor Force Statistics from the Current Population Survey, 2016). The number of hours Americans work has increased substantially in the past 40 years. In fact, the US Department of Labor estimates that in 2013 Americans worked almost a month more a year than they did in 1979 (Mishel, 2013).

Government is gridlocked and offers little hope of improving the lives of most Americans. Nonprofits do not have the resources, scale or impact to move the needle enough to create the changes we need.

Now, the greatest possibility for the American Dream to reinvent itself comes from the world of business. For that to happen, business must shift its thinking and how it sees itself.

Traditional Business vs. The Culture of Opportunity

Traditional Business

The predominant form of business around the globe in the early 21st century is based on a scarcity mentality and an extractive approach to wealth creation. It sees:

 Growth as defined by increased profits and status;

 The resources needed to feed that growth as existing outside of the organization and needing to be taken from the earth and from the market share of competitors;

 People as a resource to be exploited as much as possible;

 Winner-take-all competition as the road to success.

The underlying ethos is "more for me means less for you." Raw materials, money, customers, talent, technology, and new products are perceived as "out there" and must be found, bought, or controlled by any means necessary.

The *Culture of Opportunity* Process supports instead, a very different way of thinking which leads to the emergence of a new story and a new form of cooperative business.

It is a belief system based on abundance, collaboration and a generative approach to resources. It is a set of beliefs based on an opportunity mindset. It is a belief system based on understanding the sacredness of life, and our responsibility to care for the earth.

The Culture of Opportunity

Rather than seeking to control nature, it seeks to work with nature and to emulate natural processes. It sees:

 Growth as defined by conditions that support the flourishing of life in all its forms;

 The resources to feed that growth as available in the rich ecosystem of each organization, and which only need to be recognized and engaged with in a regenerative cycle that creates abundance rather than feeds on scarcity;

 People as the creative input that is as essential as capital for sustainable development, and;

 Cooperation and healthy competition as the engines that generate real value for the organization, the community and the planet.

In this new, emergent form of collaborative business, wealth is created by expansive ideas, innovative technology and robust relationships rather than by competition and dominance of scarce resources. In fact, resources grow as we make them visible, see them in different contexts and share them in new ways with other parts of our ecosystem.

The *Resource Map*, introduced later in this book, is a powerful tool within the *Culture of Opportunity* Process that empowers us to identify that wide array of resources (people, organizations, markets, capital, knowledge and communications) that is available in our environment, and recognize how their value grows as we understand their interconnectedness.

Great emergencies and crises show us how much greater our vital resources are than we had imagined.

William James, American Philosopher, Psychologist, Physician and Teacher

PART TWO

How to Build an
Opportunity-based Business

That will Thrive in Any Economy

The *Culture of Opportunity* **Process leverages the talent, relationships, knowledge, capital and communications that are largely untapped in most organizations.** We live in an increasingly connected world; within a few degrees of separation, you can find the resources you need, and you can reach your next investor, your next client or most important partnership.

The process helps you to build resilient, dynamic teams who define the results needed for healthy growth: appreciating what works well, mapping resources collaboratively and then envisioning your best year ever through a process of dialogue. One part strategic planning and one part leadership and team development, the *Culture of Opportunity* Process first focuses on short-term results and then builds the muscle needed for long-term resilience and innovation.

Rather than a formula or set of rules, the best way to think about using the *Culture of Opportunity* Process in your organization is to see yourself as a traveler who comes in with fresh eyes and an open heart. Even though you travel to your organization every day, forget what you think you know and you will discover more than you can imagine.

Step 1: Assemble Your Opportunity Team

Why you should do it:

The years leading up to, and immediately following the economic crash of 2008 was a lesson in the dangers of being insulated from reality. In my thirty years of studying business, I had never seen so many businesses, once leaders in their markets, fall so far or so fast. Seemingly rock-solid companies such as Blockbuster, Circuit City, Research In Motion, Nokia, Radio Shack, and Washington Mutual were soon out of business or greatly diminished.

What do these companies have in common? They couldn't adapt to the rapid changes all around them. They stubbornly clung to outdated beliefs. Their culture did not support challenging cherished assumptions. They failed to innovate and meet the shifting dynamic of their markets.

Resilient, enduring firms have the ability to see changes before their competitors and adapt. Their cultures are entrepreneurial and leaders are on the lookout for opportunities that will excite their customers and strengthen their business. They do this by inviting ideas and perspectives from outside of their organization. They have active and engaged boards of directors, advisory boards or, as in the case of our clients, *Opportunity Teams*.

An *Opportunity Team* is a talented and diverse mix of outside advisors and key players from inside your organization that are charged with seeking new opportunities, evaluating them quickly, and helping to launch the right ones at the most opportune time.

The outside members of the team are an essential asset to the business because they bring fresh ideas, information and practices from other industries. They are not tied to the "way we do things around here" and aren't hindered by internal politics or the fear of losing their jobs. Members of the *Opportunity Teams* we have helped our clients assemble have brought innovations from the hospitality industry to the wine business, from manufacturing to electrical supply, from Internet search to an artist's eCommerce business.

How you can do it:

Opportunity is a team sport. You can build your own *Opportunity Team* by bringing together a diverse group of people who can offer many perspectives on how to achieve sustainable success. The *Opportunity Team* provides the discipline of an outside perspective combined with the resources that allow the internal team to achieve more than they could on their own. The group you build will be key contributors to your business' new culture, so consider carefully whose contribution will be most valuable. The optimal size for an *Opportunity Team* is around seven to ten people.

A core value is that every voice is heard. During the process, formal roles and titles are dispensed with. Leaders emerge from unlikely places when given the opportunity to participate fully. Teams become stronger and more focused when they come together around shared goals, reinforcing abundance thinking and collaborating to strengthen what is already working.

To build a well-rounded team, consider including people from these three main categories:

1. **Strategic Thinkers:** People who tend to think in big, holistic terms and have some experience in helping to grow a business.
2. **Business Experts:** People who are experts in areas such as strategy, operations, finance, leadership, and marketing with experience and knowledge running a business and improving key operational areas.
3. **Connectors:** People who have a large network of relationships and are generous in sharing those connections. They are people who live in a constant state of interaction with the larger world and bring new resources into your organization.

Other qualities that make highly effective team members:

STRONG *BELIEF* IN YOUR VISION

INNOVATION AND *CREATIVITY*

GENEROSITY OF SPIRIT

EMOTIONAL INTELLIGENCE

? Questions to consider:

Who do you go to when you have to debrief a critical decision or a stressful experience?

Is there anyone that has surprised you with his or her insight and creative problem solving?

What are your key strategic partnerships? Is there someone specifically aligned with your vision?

Who do you look to when you need to spread the word about something really important in your business?

Step 2: Define Your Business Resuts

Why you should do it:

One would think that the idea of defining how to measure success as a business would be such an obvious, common sense step for companies to take that we shouldn't even have to mention it. Well, strangely enough, that has not been our experience. Sure, many companies set sales and profit goals—but many do not. Very few ask the critical questions: How do we measure success? What results will give us the best chance at realizing our vision and achieving our long term goals?

Firms that focus primarily on sales and profit may find themselves successful at one moment in time and on the brink of extinction in the next. The most enduring and resilient companies measure success across multiple dimensions. These often include customer experience, employee engagement, new product development, productivity, and utilization of and return on assets or investment.

By broadening the definition of success beyond sales and profit, leaders have the opportunity to bring deeper meaning to their organizations, inspire employees and strategic partners and more fully engage customers. Your key stakeholders want to be part of a company that stands for the values in which they believe and with which they can identify.

How you can do it:

In order to measure success, you need to define it. Clarify your goals in terms of measurable and powerful results--this is the key to developing an action plan that makes a difference. Don't limit yourself to things like profits, sales, or growth. Consider the goals that lead to qualities such as employee satisfaction, environmental impact, customer satisfaction, or product development.

Engage **Your *Opportunity Team***: Put the diverse team you've recruited to work. They can help to define business results that reflect the company's mission over a 12-24 month horizon, considering the key challenges.

Conduct Quarterly Leadership Meetings: Review your business results and how you're measuring them. This is a good time to confirm that things are moving in the right direction, or an opportunity to evaluate ongoing challenges.

Maintain a Balance between the short-term and the long-term: Consider the more immediate results that your business needs to achieve with those that will keep you growing over time.

 ## Questions to consider:

Do you have strong buy-in from your team?

Take a look at the competitors or companies in other fields that you most admire; what are their measures of success?

If you were as successful as you imagine you could be, what results would your team have accomplished?

Are your business results specific and measurable?

Are your business results limited enough to allow focused action and broad enough to make them strategic and sustainable?

Are your business results aligned with your long-term vision?

Step 3: Determine Your SuccessDNA

Why you should do it:

Every company, whether great or mediocre, has a *SuccessDNA*: a set of conditions inside of the organization combined with conditions in their market under which they thrive. Great companies know their *SuccessDNA* and use it intentionally. They proactively nurture the ideal conditions inside their business and match them with those in their external environment.

Average firms aren't sure what makes them successful. For them, success appears to be random. When the *Opportunity Lab* has worked with a struggling or emerging business and helped them clearly define their *SuccessDNA* and we have shown them how to leverage it, they begin to flourish (see case study on page 115).

A classic example of the power of *SuccessDNA* and the consequences of straying from it can be found in Apple. Since it's inception, Apple had arguably been the best in the world at designing, manufacturing, and branding consumer technology that improved our lives. From the Macintosh computer to the iPad, iMac, Macbook Air, iPhone and Apple Watch, Apple has designed beautiful tools with disruptive technology that have become an integral part of their customers' lives. They are passionate about designing and building their products so that they function flawlessly and exceed their customer's expectations. They create their products in a secretive, closed environment and only release them when they are deemed perfect.

In 2012, not long after the death of Apple co-founder Steve Jobs, the company had a strange and very public deviation from their *SuccessDNA*. They kicked the web-mapping service Google Maps off of the iPhone. In its place, they released iMap, their own version of a mapping service application for iPhone. This appeared to be a hastily made decision--one which caused the app to be released well before it's capabilities had met Apple's rigorous standards--and seemed to stray from their well-established *SuccessDNA*. iMaps was resoundingly disdained by customers and its shortcomings were widely publicized on a global scale. This was the first highly visible failure of the company since losing the creative force of Steve Jobs, which led many to question the future of the once unstoppable tech juggernaut. In short order, Apple was forced to ditch iMap and restore Google Maps in its place. They had learned a powerful lesson on the importance of sticking to their *SuccessDNA*.

How you can do it:

SuccessDNA is about understanding your strengths and weaknesses so that you can pursue the ideal opportunities for you and your organization. This starts by making an honest assessment of your successes and failures over the past 3 to 5 years. You can then build on your successes by examining the processes, attitudes and actions taken that stayed consistent across these projects. Bring your best, most objective mind into this inquiry. Use the *SuccessDNA* tool found on page 115 in this book when you are ready to work through this process.

We begin the evaluation of *SuccessDNA* by asking pointed questions:

What are you best at?

What have been your most successful projects?

What have been your most significant failures?

Do your successes follow a pattern?

Are there circumstances common to your successes but not your failures?

As you get more comfortable with these questions, you will be ready to gather your *Opportunity Team*.

Choose 5 successful projects that you identified in the first step.

As a group, you will then answer the set of questions below for each project:

What was the Opportunity?

How did you identify it?

Why did you choose it?

What were the conditions inside of your organization at the time of the opportunity? (e.g., team commitment, willingness to allocate resources)

What were the conditions outside of your organization at the time of the opportunity? (e.g., market landscape, client profile)

What obstacles stood in the way of succeeding?

What internal and external resources did you use to overcome those obstacles?

What resulted from manifesting the Opportunity?

How did you measure those results?

After going through this exercise for several of your successes and perhaps one of your failures, your *Opportunity Team* is likely to see a pattern emerging.

There are factors that remain constant in your success that were not present in your failures. Having identified these conditions of success--

your *SuccessDNA*--you can now know what your company does best and what circumstances bring out your best work.

 ## Questions to consider:

Is your team being honest and thorough in responding to the *SuccessD-NA* questions?

What are your key learnings?

How can you use these insights to improve your organization?

Step 4: Build Your Resource Map

Why you should do it:

No longer are traditional institutions like government, the media and the church the most powerful forces in society. In many cases, networks are displacing them quickly. Consider the rapid and disturbing rise of terrorist groups like Al-Qaeda and ISIS. Or consider the meteoric rise of a once-obscure pop singer like Adele. Her huge fan base was not built primarily through television, radio or print advertising as it once might have been. Instead, her first record contract came after a friend posted her three-song demo to social media.

Upstart companies like Uber, AirBnB, Etsy and Warby Parker spent their venture capital not on advertising, but on creating great experiences for their customers that could then be shared enthusiastically through social networks. Rather than be centered in a physical place, they are connected by a cause or a compelling value proposition and the communication that adds glue to the network.

In an increasingly connected world of social networks like Facebook, Twitter, LinkedIN and Instagram, how can we effectively use our networks to identify and marshal the resources we need to move our business forward?

Let's use my LinkedIn contacts as an example. I have about 2000 first degree connections on LinkedIn. Using their algorithm, there are over 11 million people three degrees of separation from me. But how do I use these resources to help me build my business or advance my career? The number of contacts we have means little without the context that can help turn that connection into a genuine relationship--and eventually turn that relationship into one that is mutually beneficial.

What I have learned over the years of working in and with a broad range of businesses is that the best leaders have the ability to understand the richness and context of the resources in their networks.

People, organizations, markets, capital, knowledge, and communication exist in a connected ecosystem and acknowledging this is the key to using and sharing them effectively.

A useful example of the power of using a network of resources can be seen in immigrant populations throughout history. When I studied how my own immigrant ancestors from Eastern Europe came to thrive after their arrival to the United States, I began to understand the expansive power of social networks--or Resource Ecosystems, as we have come to call them at the *Opportunity Lab*.

The Resource Ecosystems of immigrants were and often still are centered in physical places such as specific neighborhoods within cities or towns. These are places that maintain some of the traditions and character of a particular culture. They are easy to see and to navigate, and often provide a way for newcomers to find their place within the comfort of familiar foods, language, music and customs and to establish a new life with the support of those who came before them.

In many endeavors, including the business world, we are connected via the internet rather than geography. We often can't see or touch our networks and therefore have difficulty identifying their full breadth and depth. Recognizing this need for successful leaders to visualize their networks in order to harness their full power, I began to map them. Called a *Resource Map*, we began to create them for our clients and for the *Opportunity Lab* ourselves.

The more we use and improve these maps over time, the more powerful they become. We have built *Resource Maps* that empower our clients to develop sales and marketing strategies, attract new clients, top talent and new investors.

How you can do it:

In order to understand the power of the resources you already have, you need to learn to think in terms of networks. The process starts by listing all of the key resources to which you or your organization are connected and then organizing them into the categories of people, organizations, markets, capital, knowledge and communications.

The *Resource Map* is a powerful tool that gets you to think about all of the tools and networks at your disposal differently. After working through this process, you will be able to effectively visualize and interact with your ecosystem and use it to find and implement new opportunities.

To begin, gather your *Opportunity Team* and ask some pointed questions.

 **Questions to consider:**

Who are the most important people in our resource ecosystem?

What organizations are key to our success?

What are our most important sources of capital?

What knowledge is most valuable?

How do we communicate our brand and message to our market?

As your group gets more comfortable with these questions you will be ready to use the *Resource Map* tool on page 39.

Now choose one business result that you would like to achieve as your focus for the session and answer the questions below with this goal in mind.

People:
Who are the people you know with the largest and most important social networks?

Which experts could you contact when you need critical expertise?

Which "movers and shakers" (Accelerators) could really push the needle forward?

Organizations:
Which trade and professional organizations are most important to you?

Which customer organizations are most important to you?

Which investor groups?

Which government agencies?

Which other groups?

Markets:
What markets do you operate in?

Capital:
What are your most important sources of capital?

Knowledge:

What knowledge is the most valuable to you?

Communication:
Which websites are most important?

Which social media is most important?

Which print media is most important?

Any other forms of communication?

Step 5: Imagine a Year of Opportunity

Why you should do it:

Your *Year of Opportunity* is your vision of what you now see is possible. You have started to build a *Culture of Opportunity* by bringing in the outside perspective of your *Opportunity Team*, clearly defined your business results, determined your *SuccessDNA* and created your *Resource Map*. With this new level of clarity, you can now imagine what your best year ever could be. The organizations and the leaders willing to challenge beliefs and stretch beyond what they have ever yet achieved are the ones who keep growing no matter what obstacles stand in the way.

How you can do it:

If you could create a *Year of Opportunity* from your highest and best place, with absolutely no restrictions on what is possible, what would that year look like in your professional life? In your personal life? Visualizing a *year of opportunity* helps us to establish goals and understand what we need to do in order to accomplish them.

The *Opportunity Team* will work through this exercise (see page XX in our toolkit) assuming they have no limitations and the organization is operating at its best. The team is asked: What opportunities can you create that would enhance your business results as fast and as far as you can imagine?

Each team member will share the opportunities they envision with the rest of the team. If possible, working with a facilitator can help to bring all of these potential opportunities to the full view of the group.

Organizing the Opportunities

To make more sense of the opportunities, it can help to categorize them by functional area. For example:

- Marketing and Business Development
- Product Development
- Service Delivery
- Operations
- Strategic Partnerships
- Finance
- Human Resources
- Manufacturing
- Technology

Step 6: Filter Your Opportunities To Select the Right Ones

Why you should do it:

Companies that have built vibrant, dynamic Cultures of Opportunity have an active flow of new opportunities coming their way. They have learned to use their Resource Ecosystem effectively, and they will attract far more opportunities than they could successfully execute. It is critical to filter these opportunities and select those that offer the most potential.

While Cultures of Opportunity are open and innovative, their leaders are disciplined and focused to ensure that they are successful at what they set out to do. The *Opportunity Filter* provides a simple system to select the right opportunities for a particular organization at a particular time. It requires leaders and their *Opportunity Teams* to address what projects to prioritize and what is best left for future endeavors.

Now that you and your *Opportunity Team* have developed a vision of what is possible for your organization through the *Year of Opportunity*, you are ready to begin filtering.

How you can do it:

In developing the plan to build your *Culture of Opportunity*, it is essential to choose the right opportunities quickly, discarding those that are inappropriate and tabling ones that are right but not at that time. Primary elements in the *Opportunity Filter* are the analysis of data, collaboration, and consensus.

When ready, you and your *Opportunity Team* can work through this activity on page XX in the toolkit section of this book.

Each opportunity is filtered using a sequence of questions that follow the progression of the *Culture of Opportunity* Process:

Business Results
Will this opportunity impact your business results in the timeframe needed?

SuccessDNA
Is this opportunity likely to succeed based on your *SuccessDNA*?

Note: Startup and younger businesses or a newer business unit should look to the *SuccessDNA* of their peer group.

Resource Map
Do you have the resources required to realize this opportunity?

Note: If needed resources are not on the existing *resource map*, the group can revisit their map and see how much of a stretch it would be to find these resources in their existing relationships.

Opportunity Team
Is the team on board?

Note: This is the final and arguably the most important step in the *Opportunity Filter* process. This step creates a robust and honest dialogue that not only provides the best answer for the team, but also creates the highest level of commitment to the opportunity if it is chosen and strengthens the team even if it is not.

Step 7: Turn your Vision into an Opportunity Plan

Why you should do it:

A major theme of this book has been how disorder and unpredictability have turned the world upside down. The most enduring businesses are adaptive and continually innovate in spite of the disruption around them. Those businesses also have a plan that focuses them on the right opportunities at the right time to keep their company growing. The difference between an *Opportunity Plan* and a more traditional business plan is that it is more flexible and responsive, plays to your *SuccessDNA*, leverages your Resource Ecosystem, and is created by your diverse *Opportunity Team* of people inside and outside the company .

How you can do it:

Goals are the building blocks that turn an opportunity into a reality. They are major long-term benchmarks that measure your success. Goals have a significant impact on a company or a person's future and are the first step in creating an *Opportunity Plan*.

Once goals are established they can be broken down into smaller parts, or objectives. Objectives are clear, measurable markers that assist us in achieving our goals; think of objectives as the signposts on the journey to achieving a goal. They help us to know when we are going in the right direction and when we have strayed from the path.

Why is it that some people and organizations consistently achieve their goals, enjoying success and doing the things everybody else would like to be doing? Do they do it faster? Better? One thing high-achieving individuals and organizations have in common is a clear sense of purpose and a plan to achieve it. They set measurable and meaningful objectives that tell them objectively that they are going in the right direction. The team needs to define objectives so they are accurate and effective measuring tools of the indicators that matter for sustainable success.

The objectives you set in order to achieve your overarching goals must be SMART:

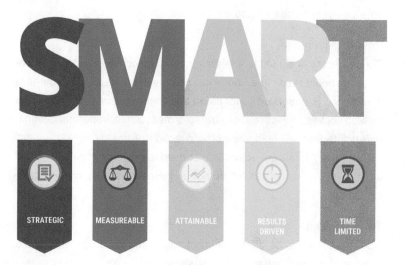

Strategic

For objectives to be truly meaningful they must lead you towards the achievement of your organizations or future goals. By strategic we mean objectives that will direct you towards long term, lasting success. The strategic goals of a company determine what objectives you should aim for. Unless objectives have a significant impact on a company's future they will not be an effective use of time and will steer you off course.

Measurable

In order to evaluate your progress, you need to be able to measure your objectives. This means that you have to put them in quantifiable terms as much as you can. For example, if your objective is to increase sales you need to determine by how much. If you are setting out to increase your knowledge base, how will you measure how much you have increased it? And remember to determine the value to the company of the objective that you have set. Using this example, you may want to identify what you could accomplish after you have gained the desired knowledge.

Attainable

For your objective to be motivating and not overwhelming, it needs to be realistic and attainable. Setting objectives that don't take into consideration the day-to-day work may be setting you up for failure. Of course, you do need to challenge yourself. Make sure that you maintain a reasonable balance between challenging and realistic.

Result-driven

Objectives are designed to achieve results. The achievement of your objectives should result in a noticeable change in an area which you have determined is important to focus on and improve. Don't confuse tasks with objectives. Objectives are strategic, measurable, important destination points that will lead you in the direction of improving your overall performance. Tasks are activities that need to be accomplished in order to achieve your objectives but do not by themselves achieve any significant result.

Time Limited

Objectives need to be driven by checkpoints and deadlines. Because a number of objectives have to be completed during a period of time, it is essential that you manage your time by scheduling how and when objectives will accomplished. Without setting specific deadlines and checkpoints to evaluate how you are doing, you won't be able to focus on your objectives or know when you are off schedule.

For further guidance as you and your *Opportunity Team* create the *Opportunity Plan*, check out the activity in our toolkit on page XX. Using the information you've gathered over the previous steps of the Opportunity Process, establish the overarching goals of your project and work your way (step-by-step) through the objectives, tasks, timelines, and responsibilities that will allow your team to achieve success. Make sure to establish a replicable but adaptable system for seizing your opportunities while they last.

Ultimately, this *Opportunity Plan* will be a major step forward in allowing you to create a true *Culture of Opportunity* with lasting impact.

Problems are only opportunities in work clothes.

Henry Kaiser, Entrepreneur and Philanthropist

PART THREE

The Culture of
Opportunity in Action

In this Part, I'll present you with three Opportunity Stories. These are case studies showing the methodology in action, demonstrating the impactful results our clients achieved from the process, along with a handful of lessons learned. Once you understand how the cultural aspects of opportunity-building work, the next two sections describe important personal refinements that might be particularly useful to you as a leader.

Opportunity Story 1

Look Forward Consulting, The Opportunity Team is a Game Changer

The Challenge

In the spring of 2016, the *Opportunity Lab* began working with Carlton Nettleton, an entrepreneur who had built a thriving consulting and training business known as Look Forward Consulting. Carlton had a vision for using his unique teaching method to train and support emerging leaders on Lean Thinking and Agile development. He helped his clients think differently about how their teams could manage complex projects by taking a more open and collaborative approach. Once accomplished on a smaller scale, Carlton aimed to grow that approach throughout an entire organization, creating a more resilient company whose employees would be more effective and less stressed.

While Look Forward Consulting worked directly with a variety of organizations, most business came through subcontracting with large training companies. In those engagements, Carlton was limited in what and how he taught and was often unable to achieve the larger goal of effecting change across an entire client organization. Subcontracting also meant that the profit margin was significantly lower, with little to no opportunity for repeat business or significant brand building.

This was the major challenge that Carlton hoped to overcome; changing the profile of his client base would substantially increase Look Forward Consulting's impact and, in turn, allow Carlton more freedom to pursue his professional and personal goals.

The Solution

We began by helping Carlton and his team get clear on the business results they needed to accomplish that would create a launchpad for long-term growth. Once established, we turned our attention to the *Opportunity Team*. While Carlton is multi-talented, with skills in program development, teaching, coaching, consulting, training and negotiating, he and his team did not have expertise in sales, marketing or finance. In situations such as these, the *Opportunity Team* is a powerful resource with the potential to help a small team gain access to new essential skills and potentially bring new competencies into the organization if members are able to commit their time.

When we began discussing the idea of an *Opportunity Team*, Carlton hadn't yet fully considered the deep and powerful relationships he had built over his career. When we arrived at the first meeting of his *Opportunity Team*, we had no idea what to expect. In addition to Carlton and his partner, Carlton had invited an entrepreneurial partner with whom he had created a video-based training program that was a core element to Look Forward's strategy, a technology entrepreneur who had built a collaboration platform used by leaders around the world, a senior technology sales leader with deep experience in Look Forward's target markets, and a colleague in Agile development outside of Carlton's region.

The group was unanimously excited to be a part of the team and to dive in with full force. They quickly helped to further refine Look Forward's business result goals and *SuccessDNA*, leading to a deeper and wider *Resource Map* and more selective *Year of Opportunity*. Using the *Opportunity Filter*, we were able to craft a robust first draft of the *Opportunity Plan* for Look Forward.

The Results

As the day was winding down I looked over at Carlton. He had a big smile on his face. He was stunned at how passionate and collaborative the team had been. Until that day, he had not realized the power of the resources he had so close to him or knew of the care and admiration the

Opportunity Team members had for him.

Toward the end of the day, after Carlton had absorbed so much feedback, he had concerns about how he would be able to act on everything. One member of his team overheard this and turned to him, looking him straight in the eye and said, "You're really competent at what you do. You are good or better than anyone I have ever worked with. You will figure it out." That comment, coupled with the outpouring of recognition for his skills and the viability of his vision, dramatically shifted Carlton's view of its business and himself.

Carlton and his partners walked away from the *Culture of Opportunity* session with:

- Clearly measurable Business Result goals
- A Success DNA profile that can leverage their ideal conditions for success
- A *Resource Map* that will help them attract clients, partners and capital they need for growth
- An Opportunity Plan to guide their growth and use of resources
- An *Opportunity Team* that provides an objective, complementary perspective of the business; adding support, insight and resources

Look Forward Consulting has already achieved success in a short period of time following the OppLab engagement, including: attracting new clients and speaking engagements, launching a second cohort of a web-based training program, and adding a full time partner to the team. We anticipate Carlton will continue down this path of success to achieve his ultimate vision of Look Forward Consulting.

Opportunity Story 2

Diana Ayton-Shenker, The Power of Business Results to Drive Action

The Challenge

Diana Ayton-Shenker, a leading thinker, writer and advisor in the social innovation community, was one of the early adopters of our *Culture of Opportunity* process. When we met, Diana was in the process of re-imagining the nonprofit project she was running called Fast Forward Fund, also and repositioning her consulting firm, Global Momenta.

At this point in her career, Diana had already achieved extraordinary success. She had held senior leadership positions at Mercy Corps, P.E.N, and Human Rights Watch and served on the board of directors of prominent national and international nonprofit organizations. She had taught Social Entrepreneurship, Corporate Social Responsibility, Organizational Management and Strategy and International Human Rights at the American University in Paris, the New School, Bard College and Hunter College. She had authored three books including A Global Agenda, about the United Nations.

Yet, with all that she had accomplished, Diana knew there was much more to be done in the social sector. There are a huge assortment of daunting social problems that need to be solved and she saw a strong need to apply the innovative approaches she had learned throughout her career. Diana decided to work with the *Opportunity Lab* to identify a clear and impactful path forward.

The Solution

Diana began by completing her *SuccessDNA* profile, *Resource Map*, and *Year of Opportunity* and was then ready to head into her first session with her *Opportunity Team*. We were working on a whiteboard, filtering the dozen or so opportunities in her *Year of Opportunity*, but then we got stuck. She paced back and forth, looking back at each of the opportunities, and became frustrated.

Several of the opportunities fit her *SuccessDNA* profile and her *Resource Map* showed her that she had access to the things that could help her realize them. However, something just didn't feel right. We reviewed each opportunity again with her *Opportunity Team*, discussing each element of the opportunity in depth.

After taking a moment to integrate the feedback she had received, her insight started to crystallize. Though the opportunities we were considering did fit with the Business Results she had defined at the beginning of the process, the level of potential impact was not aligned with her level of experience, her skill and the impact she had achieved in the past.

Recognizing this, she realized,

> *"I needed to raise the bar on the business results to focus on my highest impact opportunities. The Business Results I set were too low. When I compared opportunities to what my impact potential is, what my firm's expertise is worth, and what we have accomplished in the past, I knew I needed to reset the Business Results I wanted to achieve."*

With input from her *Opportunity Team*, she was able to get really honest with herself and become fully clear on what she wanted to accomplish. This set her on a very different path.

The Results

With enthusiastic support from her *Opportunity Team* she was able to "own" her *SuccessDNA* and expansive *Resource Map*; compelling her to increase her defined Business Results. She then defined her ideal client and developed a strategy to reach them. In time, her newly repositioned firm, Global Momenta, began to thrive.

Since Diane's *Culture of Opportunity* experience she has:

- Served as the Inaugural Nazarian Social Innovator in Residence at the Wharton School of Business;
- Served as a mentor for the Unreasonable Institute and the Clinton Global Initiative;
- Served as a strategic advisor and consultant to a number of high impact programs at organizations including the Calvert Foundation, The New School, and Ashoka;
- Been honored as one of "25 Leading Women Changing the World" (Good Business New York);
- Been chosen as one of "31 Inspiring Women in Nonprofit Management" (UNC), and featured on the World Economic Forum agenda.

Opportunity Story 3

Mapos, The Power of Owning Your Unique Greatness

The Challenge

Mapos, an innovative sustainable architecture and design firm, came to the *Opportunity Lab* in 2013 with the goal of thinking more consciously about their next stage of growth. Partners Colin Brice and Caleb Mulvena had some success in the first five years of Mapos' existence, yet they knew they had even greater potential. In their early years, they took the projects they could get and made the best of them, as many start-ups must do. While this brought in revenue and a list of satisfied clients, allowed them to hire staff and helped them to build a body of work, it was not always fully aligned with their passion. This work also did not efficiently leverage their talents or network of resources.

I first met Colin at an event in Yonkers, where I learned about his passion for reusing building materials, equipment and furniture abandoned by a society that often neglects the historic value and quality of these items. Colin, a native of Ohio, grew up seeing this lack of reverence for craft, history and community ravage the once vibrant, innovative urban centers of Cleveland and nearby Detroit. In turn, he has witnessed and participated in its resurgence, using design-thinking and a respect for the power of placemaking to reinvent a city. After meeting Caleb, I quickly saw that these two men wanted to bring their passion and their unique take on how business, community, design, brands and their environments could be reimagined to a wider audience.

The Solution

Our first step was to help Colin and Caleb define their *SuccessDNA*: what made each of them and their firm uniquely great. We took a deep dive into the five most successful projects they had accomplished since the founding of Mapos. We looked at the conditions inside the organization and in the marketplace during each project. They became energized by naming and then owning the conditions under which they excelled.

Their *SuccessDNA* combined a deep caring about their collaborative partnership with clients with rock solid experience in green building, sustainability and the adaptive reuse of materials. They thrived when working with clients who shared their values and were highly responsive and cost-competitive in the most challenging economy.

When we got to their *Year of Opportunity* and began to filter each opportunity through the four *Opportunity Filters* (Will it impact your business results in the time you need it to? Do you have the resources to achieve it? Is it consistent with your *SuccessDNA*? Does your team believe in it?) there was a moment of truth. Building and running a boutique hotel in upstate New York was one of the opportunities they had defined. They were really passionate about this idea, and they already had a vision for it.

When the questions arose about how this fit with their *SuccessDNA*, they stopped and took a breath. Clearly, it did not. Moreover, if they tried to expand their *SuccessDNA* by adding resources through their *Resource Map*, it would risk distracting them from realizing the opportunities that did make it through the *Opportunity Filter*. The Mapos team chose to stay focused.

The Results

Following their experience with the *Culture of Opportunity* process, Mapos has experienced consistent and substantial growth. This in turn has allowed their *SuccessDNA* to grow, and Mapos was able to return to the hotel opportunity. The team has now successfully designed two boutique hotels, including one in upstate New York. Many other projects have since come their way, resulting in major media coverage in *The New York Times, The Wall Street Journal, Contract Magazine, Architect Magazine* and *The Architect's Newspaper.*

Through the *Culture of Opportunity* program, Colin and Caleb learned some precious life lessons about running a business that would support their values and personal goals and thrive despite a volatile economy.

"Everything and anything is an opportunity. Make sure you uncover all of the resources in your network. Sometimes, they come from surprising directions," said Colin, when we talked three years after our last session.

It was gratifying to learn that many central principles of our work together had become a part of the guiding principles of Mapos. "It is always exceptionally beneficial to get out of the office and look at the big picture. Since working with OppLab, we have made a partners retreat an annual ritual. We also have disciplined ourselves to meet every Monday to work on improving the business and handling people and operational issues as they arise. We also decided to focus only on projects that reflect our values."

Mapos partners Colin and Caleb came away from their *Culture of Opportunity* process having attracted new, profitable business that fits their *SuccessDNA*, including:

- A major redesign of Tom Colicchio's 'Wichcraft fast casual restaurant chain
- A concept design for cosmetics retailer Fresh, including stores in China, South Korea, North America and Europe
- The New York City office design and retail concept design in China, Paris and London for privately owned beauty brand, Caudalie
- The design of the LivePerson Headquarters in New York with adaptive reuse of materials and furniture and regional offices in Atlanta and San Francisco
- The renovation of Hotel Shogard, which turned an abandoned single room occupancy hotel into a boutique gem with renovation, rebranding and repurposing of marquee, signage and materials
- The restoration of Republic Restoratives, an abandoned warehouse in Washington, DC that was turned into a distillery and lounge, supporting the renaissance of an urban core neighborhood

When I let go of what I am, I become who I might be.

Lao Tzu, Author of the I Ching

PART FOUR

Principles for Conscious Leaders

Tonya Surman, Co-Founder and former CEO of the Centre for Social Innovation/Canada, inspires the CSI/NYC community

Cultures of Opportunity are new and evolving forms of organization. They will grow and evolve as leaders within them grow and evolve. Relationships and social networks will develop that will support these leaders and these new kinds of organizations. Cultures of Opportunity are conscious entities; they are created by a clear purpose and strong, resilient values. These new and radically different types of organizations will require a very different kind of leader. They will not be the Alpha Male CEO. In fact, COO leaders will come from anywhere and everywhere in the organization. They may not even have a formal leadership title. What they will possess is an intense curiosity and willingness to learn, particularly in learning about themselves, their associates inside and outside of the organization and the disruptive world around them.

For me, these three principles have helped me and many of the leaders I work with develop the ability to see the world through a broader, more inclusive lens. To lead more through sharing, supporting and inspiring rather than commanding.

Principle 1: The Greater Good

One of the important principles for conscious leaders building successful and sustainable businesses is what I have come to call "The Greater Good." As we move from a culture based on scarcity and competition into a culture of abundance and collaboration, our leaders need to develop the language, actions and beliefs that support this shift. This includes the belief that doing well in service of our own interests must also include working toward the Greater Good with our families, communities and organizations..

For me, this change in mindset needs to begin by understanding the concept that life is sacred. For decades, America's version of capitalism did not account for the many lives impacted by business in which the sole purpose was maximizing profits for its shareholders. As Nobel Laureate economist Milton Friedman stated, "There is one and only one social responsibility [of a business]-to use its resources and engage in activities designed to increase its profits so long as it stays within the rules of the game, which is to say it engages in open and free competition without deception or fraud." What Friedman and several generations of business leaders overlooked was the collateral damage of ignoring the needs of other stakeholders in the ecosystem of a business.

When employees, customers, communities and the environment are treated as non-entities, it sets society on a dangerous course of competition between key segments of society. Life is not seen as sacred. Corporations are perceived to be succeeding at the expense of society. However, this philosophy of profit over people has started to change. Michael Porter, Harvard professor, best-selling author of Competitive Strategy and arguably the most important thought leader on business strategy, began to shift his view of the place of business in society over the past decade.

In 2011 he published a groundbreaking article in the Harvard Business Review, co-authored with Mark Kramer, called Creating Shared Value: How to reinvent Capitalism and unleash a wave of innovation and growth.

In it, they argue that in order for businesses to be successful and sustainable they need to shift their beliefs about how they create value and their responsibility for society at large.

> When employees, customers, communities and the environment are treated as non-entities, it sets society on a dangerous course of competition between key segments of society.

There is a need to stop measuring success through the narrow lens of short-term profit and expand it to the broader influences on long-term success. So, what does this mean for us? If we want to help lead this shift in how we view business we need to begin with ourselves. Each one of us can actively struggle with the questions: What is the Greater Good for our team? For our company? For our industry? We must internalize the idea that work for the good of the group benefits us to really see the benefit of working for both. As in the well-worn phrase, "a rising tide lifts all boats," you will make your boat the most seaworthy it can be while simultaneously helping the tide to rise.

At the *Opportunity Lab*, where we are a Founding Member of the Centre for Social Innovation (CSI), a collaborative workspace and incubator for social entrepreneurs and nonprofits in New York City, we continually look for ways that our activities can benefit CSI, ways in which CSI's activities can benefit us, and how we can work together. We serve on committees, co-create programs with CSI staff and other members and help to bring resources to our community. We also understand the need for focus and balance. There are many times when we need to put our resources to work in areas unrelated to CSI. We believe, over time, the Greater Good of a stronger *Opportunity Lab* will serve the Greater Good of the Centre for Social Innovation community.

Action Steps

If you would like to begin exploring the idea of the Greater Good and begin implementing it in your business, here are a few simple steps:

Step 1: Reflection

Set aside a specific time for the next month to explore this critical principle for yourself and with your team and colleagues. "What is the Greater Good for our team? For our company? For our industry? For our clients, customers, partners?" Then ask "What could we change in how we work that would support Doing Well by Doing the Greater Good?" Then look for opportunities to put these new ideas into practice.

Step 2: Assessment

For a more in depth exploration in the Greater Good, you can learn a tremendous amount from the work Michael Porter, Mark Kramer and their colleagues have done at FSG Consulting, a firm whose mission is to re-imagine social change. Their Shared Value Readiness Assessment is a powerful tool to see where you and your group are in your beliefs and practices around Creating Shared Value, which is a specific methodology for enacting the Greater Good.

Step 3: Action Plan

If you find the Assessment tool as useful as we did, then consider bringing your team together to develop an Action Plan based on the results of your reflections and the assessment. Take some time with the Action Steps which can be guided by the questions and links to additional resources in the assessment.

Resources

Article
Creating Shared Value: How to reinvent Capitalism and unleash a wave of innovation and growth. Michael Porter and Mark Kramer, Harvard Business Review 2011

Video
Creating Shared Value Readiness Assessment video http://www.fsg.org/tools-and-resources/shared-value-readiness-assessment

Website
The Greater Good: Science for a Meaningful Life http://greatergood.berkeley.edu/ Articles, videos, research and news from the world recognized University of California at Berkeley Greater Good organization.

Principle 2: Change Your Belief to Change Your Future

During several decades of working with entrepreneurs and business leaders to help them grow their businesses and determining how to grow my own, I have seen a spectrum of results from resounding success to heartbreaking failure.

The people I admire the most are those who understand that in order to grow their business, they themselves must grow. When things go wrong, they don't look to blame others. Instead, they become introspective. They look to improve their emotional intelligence, attitude, confidence and resolve any inner conflicts that hold them back.

In addition, they look to enhance their technical skills and their ability to listen, to receive feedback, to collaborate and to lead their organizations.

> The people I admire the most are those who understand that in order to grow their business, they themselves must grow.

The one area of development that has been the most critical for inner growth has been belief. Tye Atwood, Chief Operations Officer at one of our client companies, once told me about the impact of the collective belief of an organization on the results it produces: "We got to where we got because we think how we think." Whenever I see a business that has hit a plateau, or is unable to solve a significant problem, I have found through painstaking investigation that the path to an effective solution comes through changing what and how we think about the situation we are in. In other words, we change what we believe.

In the process of reflecting on the changing lessons I have learned that led to the writing of this book, a number of core beliefs have come into focus. The first, and maybe the most difficult, has to do with collaboration and competition.

From the age of 8, I was trained as an athlete. This was an era (1960s) when competition felt very primitive and survivalist. A quote of Vince Lombardi's, the iconic head coach of the Green Bay Packers, became etched in my brain: "Winning isn't everything, it's the only thing".

To me, collaboration was only relevant in pursuit of winning. If our team didn't win, we were taught to then look within our team to see who hadn't done his job and implore them to get it right.

The shame of losing was so painful because the sole focus was on improving my performance and motivating my teammates to improve theirs.

Competition in sports, and later in school, business, and later all of life was a winner take all affair.

As my life in sports and school shifted to career and personal relationships, the beliefs I learned in sports became confusing and painful. Through a series of frustrating experiences using competitive thinking in situations that would have been much better suited to a collaborative approach, I began to transform my beliefs.

This concept became my focus following a major catastrophe in my life.

In 1981, our home was nearly destroyed in a fire--we needed to create a collaborative team to help us to rebuild.

Living in a home with no heat, no hot water, no electricity, no windows and no kitchen set the clock furiously ticking in my head. I wanted to make as much progress as possible each day while spending as little money as possible. My crew, consisting of my brother-in-law, a close friend, a handful of helpers and contractors, were highly motivated to help my wife and me. However, naturally they also wanted to make money, feel good about helping out and not exhaust themselves so they could live the rest of their lives.

I quickly saw that dictating deadlines or any form of pressure was useless. I turned to the skills I had learned during my years in social work: observing, listening and seeing the world through the lens of systems. I realized the most important time of the day was when the work was done and we celebrated with a cold beer, a game of darts and savoring what we had accomplished. Now my emphasis was on supporting the guys by giving them everything they needed to do their best work and enjoy the camaraderie of accomplishment. This meant making sure they had their tools and supplies, music they liked, plenty of their favorite food and the right atmosphere to enjoy themselves when the workday was done.

Within one week we had heat, light and working bathrooms. Within a month, we had new windows and bedrooms without dirt and soot. By six months, we had a newly painted and alarmed house and much of the smell of fire was gone. By eight months, we had a new kitchen. What at first had felt like an overwhelming disaster became transformed into a life lesson. My beliefs about the conditions under which people and groups work best had forever changed.

Action Steps

If you would like to begin discovering and shifting beliefs that no longer support your business, here are a few simple steps:

Step 1: Reflection

Set aside a half hour per week, or more if needed, for the next month. Ask yourself: "What is not working in my business? What beliefs might be causing conditions that no longer work?" Then ask, "What new belief would support that part of my business?" Look for opportunities to put that new belief into practice.

Step 2: Assessment

For a deeper dive into your beliefs and how they affect your business, take our Conscious Leadership Assessment. You will find this in depth assessment on page 100 of the Toolkit. It provides a self-assessment that addresses topics such as attitude and state of being, health and wellness, relationships and community and organizational leadership and support.

Take your time with this powerful tool. When you have completed the Assessment phase, read through the answer key which will guide you in taking what you have learned and turn it into positive action to improve your business and your life.

Step 3: Belief Change Process

Morty and Shelly Lefkoe, founders of the Lefkoe Institute and creators of the Lefkoe Method, have spent over three decades studying beliefs and how to change them. The Lefkoe Method can be done online through a video-based program or via Skype. Shelley Lefkoe will lead you through a series of steps to uncover unsupportive beliefs, removing their power to hold you back and then shifting your belief to support your current intention. I have used both the video-based method and Skype sessions several times with excellent results. Go to recreateyourlife.com/free to try the video program or contact the Lefkoe Institute for more information.

Resources

Books

Mindset: The New Psychology of Belief by Carol Dweck Ph.D., World renowned Stanford University psychologist. Through decades of research on achievement and success, Dr. Dweck has discovered a groundbreaking idea-the power of mindset.

Relevant TED Talks

Grit: The Power of Passion and Perseverance by Angela Duckworth. Duckworth's popular TED talk challenges beliefs about success and competence. You will likely be inspired and informed by this powerful talk. It builds on the work of Carol Dweck and her theory of the growth mindset.

The Psychology of Your Future Self by Dan Gilbert. Gilbert, best-selling author and Harvard psychologist. He says our beliefs about what will make us happy and effective are often wrong — a premise he supports with intriguing research, and explains in his accessible and often humorous books and talks.

Principle 3: The Quiet Mind of the Conscious Leader

The task of building a successful, sustainable business is formidable. Ensuring that your business continues to evolve and adapt to the many and sometimes jarring changes that it will face can be downright daunting.

How do leaders provide the emotional intelligence, insight, compassion, resilience and strength required?

More and more leaders, including me, are turning to meditation and mindfulness.

> When I look back on my career, I recall how I was able to manage many stressful and sometimes even traumatic events much more effectively because of my meditation practice.

I was inspired to strengthen my meditation practice by committing to two 20-minute sessions a day after reading Russell Simmons' bestselling book on meditation, Success with Stillness. At the Wisdom 2.0 for Business Conference in 2014, I learned how one employee at BlackRock, the world's largest investment firm, started a meditation practice with one small group and it organically spread to over 10,000 employees. It further convinced me of the power of meditation in business.

Multiple research studies have demonstrated that meditation has the ability to decrease anxiety hence potentially increasing resilience and performance under stress. Recently, the CEO of one of our clients began to practice transcendental meditation. I have been able to notice that the practice has improved his ability to focus, stay calm under pressure and balance the demands of growing and complicated business.

When I look back on my career, I recall how I was able to manage many stressful and sometimes even traumatic events much more effectively because of my meditation practice. This book and the birth of the Opportunity Lab would never have come to light without my meditation practice.

I typically meditate within 10 minutes of waking and during the evening, preferably several hours before I go to sleep. In the morning, meditation helps me process the experience I have when waking up. Any dreams I might remember, emotions I might be experiencing and insights about the day to come get cleared through this period of silence.

For me, meditation is reaching the silent witness inside of myself. I can watch my mind from a distance that blocking outside stimuli provides, quiet it and see beyond what the ego driven mind can't see.

During my evening meditation, I am able to slow down and quiet the furious onslaught of thoughts (researchers say between 60,000 and 80,000 per day) provoked by the activities of the day.

Fears, frustrations and desires are calmed. The furious clock ticking with inner demands slows and turns into an intention of how I want to use the remaining time I have that day. Often, an experience of gratitude emerges as my mind quiets and a deeper place inside of me is touched.

If you are interested in how meditation benefits leaders, the following are some action steps to help you get started and some resources I recommend if you'd like to learn more.

Action Steps

Step 1: Set an intention for Daily Meditation

Over time, meditation sessions twice a day for twenty minutes each is ideal according to a number of research studies. However, whatever works best for you is what I recommend. The most important thing is to get started in the way that will motivate you to keep the practice going.

Step 2: Find a Quiet Place and Time
Where You Feel Comfortable

Because your intention is to quiet your mind, you want to keep the outside stimuli to a minimum. Remove all of your devices from the place you choose to meditate. Minimize outside noise and light. Wearing a sleep mask can be helpful. Find a comfortable position with your back straight and feet flat on the floor.

Step 3: Begin by Closing Your Eyes and
Taking a Deep Cleansing Breath.

There are two prominent schools of meditation-Vipassana [which focuses on the breath] and TM [short for Transcendental Meditation which uses a mantra]. Both can be highly effective. If you prefer breath, breath in through your nose for a count of 4 and out through your nose for a count of 6. If you prefer a mantra, chose a simple sound with no specific meaning, like OM. Focus on that. If a visual cue is easier, you can use a point on the wall or the light of a candle on which to focus.

What is most important to remember is that the consistency of your meditation practice is what brings you the greatest benefits. Research has shown that how much you are thinking during meditation does not diminish the benefits of meditation. It is called a practice because quieting your mind and reaching a place of calm and peace takes repetition and reflection.

Resources

1. Harvard Business Review article "How Meditation Benefits CEO's" by Emma Seppala, published December 14th, 2015
2. TED Talk:"All It Takes Is 10 Mindful Minutes" by Andy Puddicombe
3. Success with Stillness by Russell Simmons

There is no more strategic issue for a company, or any organization, than its ultimate purpose. For those who think business exists to make a profit, I suggest they think again. Business makes a profit to exist. Surely it must exist for some higher, nobler purpose than that.

Ray Anderson

PART FIVE

Conclusion: The Challenges of Scale

We've nearly reached the end of the *Culture of Opportunity*. I hope in some sense, I've inspired you to give these ideas a try. I believe they are too important to be left unnoticed. In this book I have outlined the daunting impact of the Age of Disorder on how businesses operate. You have seen how having a long term vision and a plan to execute it is not enough in this unpredictable world. When we think we can predict the future and count on our plans, we have taken a giant step towards becoming irrelevant.

You've been offered the *Culture of Opportunity* as an alternative model that enables your company to discover, evaluate and launch the right opportunities to keep your business growing regardless of the state of the economy. You have walked through a step-by-step process that will help you nurture an opportunity mindset until it becomes ingrained in your organization's DNA. I have shared three Opportunity Stories that show our process in action and the powerful results that can come from it.

We, however, aren't quite finished with our work together. I have one more critical idea that I want to explore with you-the challenge of scale. After all, what good is a *Culture of Opportunity* unless you can grow it in a way that best suits your company? Here we go....

> Owning your own business offers the promise of controlling your destiny, the ability to do things the way you want and the opportunity to earn the money you deserve.

If you look at the percentage of businesses that fail in their first five years, you might wonder why so many of us start companies in the first place. The reason, I suppose, is America's fierce and enduring entrepreneurial spirit. Although the U.S. now ranks 12th in the number of new business started each year among developed nations – it used to rank 1st – it still creates about 400,000 new businesses every year (Morelix, Fairlie, Russell, Reedy, & Tareque, 2016).

Owning your own business offers the promise of controlling your destiny, the ability to do things the way you want and the opportunity to earn the money you deserve. It is something you can choose to pass on to your children or your employees. Most importantly, it provides the opportunity to make a difference.

For many entrepreneurs, however, this intriguing promise ends in the business either failing outright or simply failing to meet its owner's needs. Alternatively, it succeeds at meeting many of the owner's needs, yet never reaches its full potential. Why? My experience points to two primary reasons.

The Power of Unconscious Beliefs

First, the entrepreneur is not able to align her needs and values with those of customers, employees, and other stakeholders. When she starts the business, the aspiring entrepreneur is often so focused on what she wants to do that she spends too little time understanding the needs, resources and common practices of her customers, employees and other stakeholders.

This lack of understanding unintentionally creates misalignment. Let me give you an example of what I mean.

About 10 years ago I met an extraordinary artist, Rena. She was one of the world's most acclaimed lighting designers, having had major installations in New York, Edinburgh, Rome, and other major cities. Rena had taught at prestigious universities, including Harvard, Parsons, and the School of Visual Arts, and presented at prominent conferences. Yet, to my astonishment, she could barely pay her bills and worked out of a dank basement with two part-time staff and a handful of freelancers, all of whom were very loyal to her.

When we began working together, we uncovered a few core beliefs that had led to serious dysfunction in her business. She did not believe that her clients would pay her enough to build her business. She did not believe she could attract and pay for the right staff, so she could free herself to focus on the truly unique, creative work that only she could do. Deep down, she did not believe she deserved success. She did not possess an opportunity mindset.

As we uncovered these beliefs—and helped her look at them objectively— she was able to shift to a more empowering belief system. Subsequently, she attracted new clients, raised her fees, hired a few full-time staff, moved into a bright functional office, and began enjoying her work again.

This impressive growth continued for a few years until she hit a wall. When I encouraged her to identify her *SuccessDNA*, the projects and clients that were the most successful for her, and then build an Ideal Client Profile, she resisted.

Her focus was on how frustrating or financially challenged her clients were and how difficult it was to manage her staff. By staying embedded in her frustration, she stayed away from what was really holding her back – her beliefs. Although her beliefs had changed dramatically and her business had grown substantially, she had imposed an unconscious limit on its growth and, in turn, her happiness. Her opportunity mindset needed to grow in order for her business to scale.

Beneath her surface reasoning she did not believe that her customers, her employees, and she could all get their needs met. She believed, as many entrepreneurs and business leaders do, that there is an inherent conflict between these groups of stakeholders. When you hold this belief you can never create an alignment in which customers, employees, owners and other primary stakeholders all win.

Key Stakeholders are Central
to Enduring Success

Such misalignment is at the core of many business failures as well as the plateauing of organizations that do not reach scale. Even many successful companies struggle with this idea. The gospel of American capitalism is the shareholder comes first and the customer, in theory, a close second. However, customers' needs are often fulfilled only when they ultimately benefit the owners. Employees, communities, the environment and sometimes even customers are often seen as disposable entities to be given only what is required for them not to be obstacles. We have seen too many instances where customers' wants are fulfilled to make a profit without any thought to their real needs. Too many exploding cars, risky mortgages and recalled pharmaceuticals are evidence of this.

In a true opportunity culture, conscious leaders seek to maximize what their business provides to all primary stakeholders. They understand for their business to be sustainable and reach its full potential, all stakeholder groups need to have a mutually beneficial relationship with their company.

Let's go back to our brilliant lighting designer. Realizing the limits of her belief system and the daunting challenge of bringing any business to the appropriate scale, she joined a much larger, global firm where their expertise and resources could help her realize her true greatness. Rena was truly a conscious leader in her high level of awareness of her skills, her needs and her limitations. It was a happy ending, though rare for entrepreneurs who can't achieve alignment and scale to find another route. By scale, I don't mean growth for growth's sake, which is too often the result of our seemingly insatiable appetite for growth at all costs. My definition of appropriate scale is centered around an organization's commitment to reach its potential so that it can sustainably add the best possible value to its customers, associates, communities, suppliers and owners.

Founders Beliefs Must Shift to Free the Business to Grow

The second reason why business owners fail to reach their full potential is that they fail to grow in order for their businesses to grow. Because a business is such an intimately personal expression of the entrepreneur, it requires the founder to see herself in a very different way as the business grows.

In my time working with founders, I've learned that the behaviors that make entrepreneurs successful initially can also undercut their ability to run larger businesses. Their challenge is not that they have an unsuitable personality for leadership. It's that their beliefs have not changed to allow the business to expand beyond their immediate reach. A founder who can scale is able to discard the habits and skills that once helped them succeed yet have outlived their usefulness.

There are three beliefs that often work for founders of small companies, yet become major stumbling blocks when those same entrepreneurs try to lead larger organizations with more diverse needs, departments, challenges, and stakeholders and a build a *Culture of Opportunity*:

The first belief has to do with the founder's loyalty to her first followers. This usually tightknit band of colleagues who are there when the doors open first engender a deep sense of gratitude, often indebtedness. This unyielding loyalty can become a significant liability as the organization grows. Surely loyalty needs to be respected and rewarded. As the organization grows, the founder's original team, just like the founder herself, needs to be evaluated objectively. Either they must develop skills as the business requires or transition out. In Rena's case, she had relied completely on a small, tightknit group of part-time employees and free-lancers who reinforced her beliefs and were very set in their approach to serving clients. No new ideas were flowing into her company. As she expanded her team to be larger and more diverse, innovation became a greater part of her firm's culture. Some of the original team stayed and some left.

The second belief, the need to have a singular focus, is an important attribute in a visionary who wants to unleash a revolutionary product or service on the world. Yet this quality can harden into tunnel vision if the leader can't become more expansive and see the bigger picture as the company grows. When the business is just starting out, having a laser-like attention on the project of the moment is essential for ensuring proper execution. When a leader works so close to the ground in a larger organization, however, she will eventually lose sight of the bigger picture. Rena was so narrowly focused on working in the business; on the few of the most innovative or high profile projects she was leading, she allotted little time to work on the business. As her beliefs shifted and she and her staff developed effective systems, her time was freed up to focus more on the future.

> A leader whose business reaches its full potential can reframe these beliefs by a strong commitment to self-awareness and requesting feedback from others.

The third belief, that it is better to work in isolation, is fine for the brilliant innovator who works on one project at a time. But it's ineffective for a leader who wants to build a world class organization that can scale. For Rena, she preferred to develop her ideas on her own, and later, when they were fairly well fleshed-out, she would share them with her team. When ideas and the projects they generate are developed in isolation, they lose the benefit of alternative views and creative input before they are fully formed. As Rena became more confident in her team and the collaborative process, she involved more of the creative talent in her firm much earlier on. The projects not only became more innovative, they also became more efficient in their execution.

A leader whose business reaches its full potential can reframe these beliefs by a strong commitment to self-awareness and requesting feedback from others. She is open to shifting her views and behaviors. She confronts problems directly and when necessary, supports nonperformers being moved out of the organization. She sees past distractions and establishes strategic priorities. She makes concerted, sometimes uncomfortable, efforts to do what doesn't come naturally for the team's sake. She learns to work with and communicate with diverse employees, customers, and external constituencies. Most importantly, she makes the company's continuing health and welfare her top concern.

Sustainable Scale Comes from Recognizing the Interest of the Two Most Ignored Stakeholders

The most difficult of the stakeholder groups to align with are the community and the environment. Communities where companies do business have mostly lost their say in what businesses do that affect them. From the environmental impact of a company's activities to their use of its transportation systems, its schools (for educating employees and their children) to health care, the police, the fire department, mail and other public services; there is no accepted ethos that business should be responsible for or engaged in the life of its communities. If Cultures of Opportunity are to flourish and make a difference in our world, this must shift.

Lastly, the overall environment consequences of a business's endeavors are extremely difficult to measure. They exist nonetheless. One of the first companies in America to accept responsibility for its relationship with communities and the environment is Interface — a global leader in design, production and sales of environmentally-responsible modular carpet for the commercial, institutional, and residential markets, based in Atlanta, Georgia.

How the Father of American Sustainability Did the Impossible

I met Ray Anderson, the patriarch of the sustainability in business movement in the spring of 2010 at a conference at the United Nations. Towards the end of the day I heard a man talk about the moment that changed his life and, for me, that speech would change mine. After his talk, I introduced myself and thanked him for the important work he was doing. It was a handshake and a smile and then he was gone. His warm Georgia smile and gentle patrician's manner left its mark on me.

By 1994, Ray Anderson's company, Interface, was twenty-one years old and far more successful than he ever imagined it could be. In just 18 years, Ray has lead Interface into the Fortune 500. Then, seemingly out of the blue, he heard about a customer in Southern California that asked his Interface sales rep what the company was doing about the environment.

When that question got back to Ray, he responded in disbelief: "What does he mean, what are we doing? We comply with the law. What else are we supposed to be doing?"

Listening to the Customer Drives Change

So, after two decades in business; after risking his life savings, his reputation, losing his first marriage; it hadn't troubled Ray one bit that "his company consumed enough energy each year to light and heat a city. Or that we and our suppliers transformed more than a billion pounds of petroleum-based raw materials into carpet tiles for offices and hospitals, airports and hotels, schools, universities and stores around the world. So what if each day just one of my plants sent six tons of carpet trimmings into a local landfill? What happened to it there? It was someone else's problem, not mine....In fact our belching smokestacks, our gushing effluent pipes, our mountains of waste (All completely legal) were tangible proof that business was good. They meant jobs. They meant orders coming in, products going out, and money in the bank." (Anderson, 2009)

Ray couldn't imagine that his company would ever be big enough to have a material negative impact on the community or the greater environment.

Yet, he never forgot that his customers' belief in him and his company was the reason for his success.

He never forgot the day that he had his first factory built, people hired and trained, raw materials in the warehouse, and not one order yet on the books. That experience seared into the core of his being the importance of listening to the customer even if you didn't like what they had to say. Every order represented the next heartbeat of the company. Here is one customer asking something they hadn't ever considered. Ray wondered if one customer bothers to inquire about the environment, who knows how many others are thinking about it and not asking. Somebody needed to come up with an answer.

Jim Hartzfeld, a young, recently minted MBA, was assigned to create the task force to develop that answer. So yes, it was off Ray's desk, though only temporarily. Jim asked Ray to kick off the task force to give his environmental vision. Ray was famous for saying that he didn't have an environmental vision. The point is that he had not considered the other stakeholders such as the environment and the greater community beyond the customer and satisfying the order.

Then, returning to his office to write the speech that he did not want to write, he spotted a book on his desk. It wasn't one of his, and he had no clue who had put it there-it was *The Ecology of Commerce* by Paul Hawken. He stared at the book for a moment. He began thumbing through it. It got his attention, he read on. What he found was an indictment.

> *"According to Hawken (who had built a business, the Smith and Hawken garden supply firm from scratch) our planet...was in terrible danger. Every place you looked-the oceans, the air, the forests, the farmland....were in decline.....the prime suspect? The culprit? Why, it was business. It was industry, it was corporations just like mine, taking from the earth, using resources inefficiently, generating pollution, sending more and more stuff out of our factories into the world just to end up in landfills or burned up in incinerators, forcing the earth to absorb things we used only briefly and then threw away."* (Anderson, 2009).

Values Provide the Strength to Transcend Your Ego

This is what Ray came to call his "Spear in the Chest" moment. He indicted himself as a plunderer, a destroyer of the earth, a thief stealing his own grandchildren's future and in so doing eroding the very foundation of commerce itself.

Here he was, sixty years of age, having built a publicly traded global enterprise with dozens of plants selling modular carpet in 110 countries. Imagine that for your entire adult life, you have seen yourself as an honorable man; a man who has built a business that has created thousands of jobs, invested money into dozens of local communities, provided investors with a solid return and given your family an extraordinary life. Now, in a blinding flash of insight, you are not that person anymore. You are a very different person. Not a good corporate citizen but a villain.

Not someone who will leave an admired legacy but someone who is now afraid he may die with a crushing sense of guilt. His former ideal self, wiped away by a reality he had had no access to.

So, how did Ray Anderson respond after receiving the Spear in his Chest? Ray was a man of faith. For years, he had taught Sunday school in his local Methodist church. Doing right by God was central to his sense of himself. Now, he had come to see himself as a sinner, a fallen man-and he had to right that.

Jim Hartzfeld, the man who pushed him to face the environment issue rather than run from it, told me, "It was a road to Damascus moment." Ray Anderson, with his ferocious optimism, would quickly come to see this as just another challenge, another opportunity to rise to a higher purpose. That purpose was not only to make his company a shining example of environmental stewardship, but to make that environmental stewardship a unique and permanent business advantage. Jim remembered that, "there was this idea back then that, if we can figure it out, this is not just a way to save the planet, this is a way to kick our competitors' asses."

Hearing the Signals through the Noise

When I read these words and heard many different versions of this moment by those close to Ray, I was deeply touched by his willingness, in the face of this soul-shattering realization, to take responsibility for his 21 years as the leader of a behemoth industrial machine. I was stunned by the hugeness of his character and what I would later discover to be the enormity of his capacity to transform his own being and the being and the actions of his company.

Ray, from his first day in business had the uncanny ability to "hear" aberrant signals in the noise of the daily business routine. Aberrant in that these signals are completely outside your current mental maps or "unconscious beliefs." He had made the transition to being able to notice potentially important new signals and to delegate their exploration to others. He also had the self-confidence and courage to allow the answers to fundamentally reshape his worldview and belief system at the short-term risk of his reputation and fortune.

Redefining the Meaning of Sustainability

Ray Anderson redefined sustainability as "doing business in ways that meet the needs of customers and the company without sacrificing the ability of future generations to meet their needs." (Anderson, 2009).

This means running a petroleum-intensive business in a manner that takes from the earth only that which is natural and rapidly renewable – not one fresh drop of oil – and to do no harm to the biosphere. In short, take nothing, do no harm.

To fully comprehend the height of the bar Ray had set, it is essential to note that he included all of the impact Interface had throughout the lifecycle of its business. This includes not only the production of carpet from its plants, but also the effect on the environment from the raw materials that made up the carpet being transported to their plants as well as the finished carpet traveling to their customers. Additionally, he considered what happened to the carpet when it was done being used. Defining the challenge in this broad and bold way could have easily overwhelmed the Interface team. Ray understood this and helped them break the quest to reach Mount Sustainability, as he came to call the challenge, into manageable chunks.

The Legacy of Ray Anderson and Interface

So, what were the results of these herculean efforts? Within six years, Interface's stock price tripled. Within fifteen years, they cut green-house gas emissions by 82%, fossil fuel consumption by 60%, waste by 66%, water use by 75%. They invented and patented new machines, materials and manufacturing processes. They increased sales by 66%, doubled earnings and raised profit margins (Anderson, 2009).

They proved, beyond any shadow of a doubt, that a global, industrial business formerly dependent on oil and waste could eliminate that dependency and subsequent damage to become much more successful and profitable business by doing so.

They would go on to inspire and guide global giants like Walmart, Unilever, UPS, Proctor & Gamble to adopt some of its practices. So, in the end, what is the legacy Ray Anderson, who died tragically of cancer in 2011? That story is still to be told. And, will largely depend on...US.

The *Culture of Opportunity* is first, and foremost an offering of love and commitment from me and the *Opportunity Lab* to all of the people who are in the communities that are working towards supporting business as a powerful driver of positive change in the world. This includes anyone who would like to join us.

As we learn how to value all life as sacred, it is my hope that we can learn how to align the needs and aspirations of all the stakeholders in the vast, interconnected ecosystem of business-customers, employees, business leaders, entrepreneurs, shareholders, suppliers, communities and the natural world.

When (if) that happens, there is no telling what an extraordinary world we can co-create.

The expectations of life depend upon diligence; the mechanic that would perfect his work must first sharpen his tools.

Confucius, Teacher, Editor, Politician, and Philosopher

The Culture of
Opportunity Toolkit

This toolkit is designed as an accompaniment to the *Culture of Opportunity* Process outlined in the earlier sections of this book. It is meant to be an ongoing resource. We hope that it will be a catalyst in helping you develop your potential, and eventually reach your goals.

There is generous space for notes, spontaneous insights and thoughts. Use it as a vehicle to help you get in touch with yourself and your unique gifts. It should be reviewed and analyzed as part of an ongoing process.

It is our intent to provide you with the tools to help you analyze your behavior and develop your own strategies for improving your effectiveness. We believe that each individual has the inherent value, creativity and ability to achieve his or her own definition of success and satisfaction.

Your power is far greater than any ideas or suggestions we can give you. It is our hope that these exercises will be a vehicle for unlocking that power.

Exercise 1: Conscious Leadership Assessment

Purpose

To help you assess your current level of competence as a conscious leader and point you towards some specific resources that can support your development.

What kind of leadership does a *culture of opportunity* require? We use the term conscious leadership because a *Culture of Opportunity* calls for a high level of awareness and intentionality. Conscious leaders understand that in order to create abundant, collaborative and resilient organizations they themselves must embody these qualities. They need to embrace self-inquiry, open-mindedness and accountability. "Be the change you wish to see in the world." This paraphrase of a quote by Mahatma Gandhi calls upon us to focus on what we can do rather than complain about what is out of our control..

Instructions

The following assessment will help you identify the attitudes and behaviors of conscious leadership and where you stand on the journey between learning and mastery. After you have completed the assessment, review the response key. It will provide you with insight to develop the attitudes and behaviors that support a *culture of opportunity*. I encourage you to suspend judgment of yourself. There is no right or wrong answer. The more objective you can be, the more you will learn.

Rate how often you agree with the statements below and circle the appropriate response.

1. I feel deep gratitude as a core experience in my life.

Always   Usually   Sometimes   Rarely   Never

2. I trust that I will get what I need in my life.

Always　　　Usually　　　Sometimes　　　Rarely　　　Never

3. I live each day with a clear sense of purpose.

Always　　　Usually　　　Sometimes　　　Rarely　　　Never

4. I feel strongly connected to all living things and the life force of the universe.

Always　　　Usually　　　Sometimes　　　Rarely　　　Never

5. I ask for help when I need it.

Always　　　Usually　　　Sometimes　　　Rarely　　　Never

6. I belong to groups where I feel nurtured and supported as a part of a community

Always　　　Usually　　　Sometimes　　　Rarely　　　Never

7. I tend to see people who work in my field as potential collaborators rather than competitors.

Always　　　Usually　　　Sometimes　　　Rarely　　　Never

8. When "bad" things happen, I look for a deeper reason or a life lesson to learn from them.

Always　　　Usually　　　Sometimes　　　Rarely　　　Never

9. I have keen insights into people and situations and trust those in-stincts.

Always   Usually   Sometimes   Rarely   Never

10. I feel confident and powerful when speaking in front of any group.

Always   Usually   Sometimes   Rarely   Never

11. My work is organized effectively so that I am very productive and efficient.

Always   Usually   Sometimes   Rarely   Never

12. What do you think you need to change inside yourself and/or your organization to be at your highest and best?

_____

_____

_____

_____

_____

_____

_____

_____

13. What specific steps could you take to support your personal and professional development?

_____

_____

_____

_____

_____

_____

_____

_____

Response Key

Question 1

Your rating on this question reflects how you view the importance of gratitude in your life. Extensive research has shown that a higher experience of gratitude leads to greater social capital and a more expansive and connected network. In turn, this means greater achievement of productivity and career goals. If you would like to improve your experience of gratitude, consider reading "The 31 benefits of Gratitude You Didn't Know About" from HappierHuman.com, a concise and powerful article on the key research and practices of gratitude. In addition, writing a five-minute-a-day gratitude journal can help you increase your awareness and increase your long-term well-being by more than 10%. Grateful leaders create grateful and effective organizations.

Question 2

The greater your sense of confidence that you can get what you need in life, the greater the chance that you will actually get it. If you rated yourself low on this question, consider looking at the work of Carol Dweck, referenced earlier in this book on page 75 . Her work clearly demonstrates how a growth mindset as opposed to a fixed mindset is the central factor in the level of success and satisfaction a person can achieve and the level of effectiveness they have as a leader. In her book *Mindset: The New Psychology of Belief*, Dweck cites a poll of 143 creativity researchers who agreed that the number one trait underlying creative achievement is exactly the type of resilience and fail-forward grit linked to the growth mindset.

Question 3

Research from the Harvard Business School tells us that fewer than 20% of leaders have a strong sense of their own purpose. The impact of this lack of clarity is often the failure to achieve our most ambitious personal and professional goals. Keep in mind there is a wide spectrum in one's clarity and commitment to purpose. Even a modest increase can make a significant difference in our levels of impact and fulfilment. If you've scored yourself as "rarely" or "never" on this question, be sure to work through the rest of this toolkit to gain some insight into your goals and create concrete action steps to achieve them.

Question 4

Our capacity to create close, meaningful relationships is another essential key to happiness, effectiveness and the ability to support cultures of opportunity. More than ever before, success in business is dependent on the success of social networks within organizations. If you scored low on this question, consider that many factors can inhibit the full experience of connectedness. Our fear of being challenged and found wanting, for example, can lead to competitiveness and ultimately viewing ourselves as separate and disconnected. Once again, even a modest improvement in our ability to connect can yield meaningful results. If you are seeking resources to help you, the TEDx Tel Aviv talk by Hedy Schleifer entitled "The Power of Connection" is one of the best tools for improving communication and connection I have ever experienced.

Question 5

One of the major roadblocks of many leaders is the difficulty we have in asking for help. Adam Grant, a professor at the University of Pennsylvania, and his best-selling book Give and Take reported on a study of people who were categorized as givers (people who freely express generosity), takers (people who are primarily concerned with their self-interest) or matchers (people who give primarily based on what they estimate they will receive) inside of various organizations. What they found showed that we seriously underestimate the potential success of those who are givers. The importance of teams and the rise of the service sector offers givers access to opportunities that takers and matchers often miss. A central insight that came from Grant's research was the clear difference between the two principal types of givers:those that give, but are reluctant to receive anything in return; and those who both love to give and to receive. Givers who are successful in both their careers and personal life tend to fall into the latter category. In the collaborative model of a *Culture of Opportunity*, leaders need to be capable of fitting this profile. They need to be able to ask for help and view this as a chance for others to give, rather than as their own weakness. If you scored on the lower end of the scale for this ability to ask for help, consider seeking out Adam Grant's book and begin thinking about opportunities in your work and everyday life in which you can both give and receive support.

Question 6

Cultures of Opportunity at their best are made up of communities of employees, customers, investors/Founders and other key stakeholders. Conscious leaders who understand the importance of building an inspired and committed community typically have a history of being active in these kinds of communities. Being "in the community" means having a sense of belonging and caring for something larger than the individual member. When an organization does not have this kind of purpose in addition to making profit or just surviving, it has to fight for its life when outside forces create pressure on it. Some of the most admired organizations such as Zappos, Ted and Starbucks have strong community cultures. They survive and often thrive through the most challenging crisis. Their leaders know how to inspire, connect and support their community. If you struggle with this, begin by thinking about the best communities in which you have been a member. What were their most outstanding traits? What did their leaders do to build and nurture those communities? What qualities within yourself can you focus on to strengthen your community?

Question 7

The path from "I" to "we" is a core aspect of a conscious leader's journey. As I discussed earlier in "Change your belief to change your future" on page 71, the capacity to transcend the ego's need to be superior through competition is a critical attribute for building a *Culture of Opportunity*,. If you scored low on this question, you may believe that competition inside of your group is healthy. In certain cases, competition between individuals and between teams to test the limits of performance is useful. More often than not, however, competition erodes trust, reduces openness, and can stifle innovation and necessary change. Ask yourself: when is competition good for me and my group? When is it not good? Are their insecurities within myself that are holding me back from being a more collaborative leader?

Question 8

The lens in which we look at the world determines how that world turns out for us. When we judge the things that happen to us as "good" or "bad", we often lose an opportunity to take an active role in shaping their impact on us and our organizations. Leaders who have the courage and commitment to build organizations that are meant to withstand the turbulence of today's world need to see beyond their immediate circumstances. When their plans don't turn out as they expected, it is important that they avoid blame or superficial answers. Most importantly, they must not take setbacks personally and instead use it as an opportunity to learn. Conscious leaders are curious, lifelong learners who spread their desire to learn from mistakes across their organization. For those who find they need to improve in this area, this form of emotional intelligence can be measured with programs like Search Inside Yourself, a great resource with public programs that can be found at siyli.org.

Question 9

The guiding principle of the *Culture of Opportunity* is seeing beyond the immediate. Very closely linked to attitude, insight is the ability to look deeper into a situation, a person or a group. Leaders and their organizations that cultivate insight accept that the world is constantly changing and that in that process things are not always what they appear to be. As with all of the principles of conscious leadership and the *Culture of Opportunity*, judgment impedes their full expression. When leaders and the groups they lead let go of judgement, they stop considering what's good or bad and begin asking themselves questions. If you rated yourself low on this question, consider a few questions. Why is this happening? What does it mean for us? How do we need to respond? Above all, we need to understand that we are living with a significant degree of uncertainty. While insight can provide clarity, true insight acknowledges we can never know everything.

Question 10

As you develop your attitude and insight, you will in turn strengthen your confidence. The more you get to know yourself and the people with whom you work, the more confident you will be in how to use your skills and experience in support of your purpose. If you rated this question with "rarely" or "never", consider that we often confuse confidence with arrogance. Unconsciously, this means that some people are hesitant to feel too confident. In my use of the word, confidence means that you believe in yourself and trust your insight and experience, yet not at the exclusion of other perspectives. In a collaborative culture, confidence is tempered by humility and respect for differences. A confident leader uses that confidence to take risks and try new approaches. Confidence and the power that can accompany leadership is not used against others to win or defeat something. When you are confident based on trusting yourself rather than as a defense against insecurities, you are open to other points of view and open to collaboration with people who have differing viewpoints. You see them as an enhancement to you rather than a threat. A good resource for those looking to build confidence is Skills You Need, a website dedicated to helping people improve life skills and the confidence to utilize them.

Question 11

Planning, identifying resources and the ability to breakdown a project into its components are key elements of being an effective leader. They are essential to the concept of acting with intention which is an overriding value in Cultures of Opportunity. Being intentional means acting with purpose. Being aware and accountable for what you want to create by focusing an organization is a core leadership skill. For those needing to improve in this area, remember that you can increase your effectiveness and the underlying principles of the organization by respecting your most important resources: your people and their time. By working to lay out the most effective way to reach your goals, you send a message of respect to your team.

Question 12

This question offers you a chance to reflect on what you have learned from this assessment and, in fact, from the entire book. Take your time and allow the insights and knowledge to be absorbed and integrated over whatever time frame makes sense to you. You may want to return several times to this exercise as your growing awareness captures new learning.

Question 13

Extensive research research shows that writing down your intentions and placing them where you can see them increases your ability to carry them out. By sharing them with others and asking for their help where needed, you can strengthen your accountability.

Exercise 2: Gratitude

Purpose

By acknowledging gratitude for what you already have, you create an abundance belief system. The more consistent and thorough your gratitude practice becomes, the more it will strengthen your capability as a conscious leader.

Instructions

Think of this as a meditation or reflection. Take some quiet time to allow what you are grateful for to arise in your mind, and then write down what comes to you.

_____

_____

_____

_____

_____

_____

_____

_____

Exercise 3: The 3 Magic Questions

Purpose

To get to know yourself and what you have to offer. The clearer you are on what you deeply care about, your special contributions to the world, and to whom you most want and need to be connected, the more able you will be to attract what you want to attract into your life.

Instructions

Take a moment to consider the things that drive you and what has the potential to make you successful.

A. What are you passionate about?

_____

_____

_____

_____

_____

_____

_____

B. What are your unique gifts?

_____

_____

_____

_____

_____

_____

_____

_____

_____

C. What groups or types of people do you connect with most?

_____

_____

_____

_____

_____

_____

_____

_____

_____

Exercise 4: Building Your Opportunity Team

Purpose

As outlined in Part Two, the *Opportunity Team* provides the discipline of an outside perspective combined with the resources that allow the internal team to achieve more than they could on their own. To build a well-rounded team, consider including people in your list from the three main categories described below.

Instructions

Strategic Thinkers

Identify people who tend to think in big, holistic terms and have some experience in helping to grow a business.

_____

_____

_____

_____

_____

_____

Business Experts

Think of people who are experts in areas such as strategy, operations, finance, leadership, and marketing with experience and knowledge running a business and improving key operational areas.

_____

_____

_____

_____

_____

_____

_____

Connectors

Consider people who have a large network of relationships and are generous in sharing those connections. They are people who live in a constant state of interaction with the larger world and bring new resources into your organization.

_____

_____

_____

_____

_____

_____

_____

_____

Exercise 5: Define Your Business Results

Purpose

To help you be fully clear on how you will measure the success of your business.

Instructions

What would you like your company to become, or develop into in the next 3 to 5 years? In other words, what is your dream or vision of your business? How would you like it to look if you could have it precisely on your terms?

_____

_____

_____

_____

_____

_____

_____

_____

What do you want the business to do for you?

_____

_____

_____

_____

_____

_____

_____

_____

What should your role in the business be in order for you to make your best contribution?

_____

_____

_____

_____

_____

_____

_____

_____

_____

What do you feel are the major obstacles standing in your way?

_____

_____

_____

_____

_____

_____

_____

_____

Additional Comments:

_____

_____

_____

_____

_____

_____

_____

_____

Exercise 6: SuccessDNA: Part 1

Purpose

To build on your successes by examining the processes, attitudes and actions taken in past projects.

Instructions

Choose one endeavor in which you have been particularly successful and answer the questions below. Repeat the exercise at least two more times and begin identifying the similarities.

Success Case Study #1

1. What was the opportunity?

_____

_____

_____

_____

_____

_____

_____

2. Why did you choose this opportunity?

_____

_____

_____

_____

_____

_____

_____

_____

_____

3. What unique gifts and skills did you use to maximize this opportunity?

_____

_____

_____

_____

_____

_____

_____

_____

4. What resources/external circumstances/situations helped you maximize this opportunity?

_____

_____

_____

_____

_____

_____

_____

_____

_____

5. What obstacles stood in the way of succeeding?

_____

_____

_____

_____

_____

_____

_____

6. How did you overcome those obstacles?

_____

_____

_____

_____

_____

_____

_____

_____

7. What were the results of manifesting the opportunity?

_____

_____

_____

_____

_____

_____

_____

_____

_____

Repeat this exercise at least twice more before moving on.

EXERCISE 6: SuccessDNA: Part 2

Purpose

To define a clear success pattern that will help you focus on opportunities that leverage your _successDNA_.

Instructions

Now, thinking about all the projects outlined in Exercise 6, consider the patterns that you see and answer the following questions.

1. What opportunities work best with you? How do you identify them?

_____

_____

_____

_____

_____

_____

_____

_____

2. What unique gifts and skills have led you to success?

_____

_____

_____

_____

_____

_____

_____

3. What resources/external circumstances have led you to success?

_____

_____

_____

_____

_____

_____

_____

_____

_____

YOUR SUCCESSDNA

Now in 1 or 2 sentences, how would you describe your _SuccessDNA_? (Try writing it a few different ways to see what works best!)

_____

_____

_____

_____

_____

_____

_____

_____

Exercise 7: Your Resource Ecosystem

Purpose

To visualize and create context for your resource ecosystem. By doing that, you can access your resources and use them to achieve your goals.

Instructions

There are 6 Key Categories of Resources that we capture during the _Re-_

source Mapping process. Any resources that you identified previously can be used here as well. Revisit the Build Your *Resource Map* section in Part Two of this book to refresh your understanding of this process if necessary.

1. People

On the *Resource Map*, People are categorized based on the how they operate in the world:

Connectors
Have large networks and love to put people together.

Accelerators
Are in a position to make things happen and move quickly towards your Ask.

Experts
'Go-To' people you can rely on for key information about a specific area of interest.

For each category, try to list 3-6 people. These may be people you know well or they may be acquaintances.

List your Connectors:

_____

_____

_____

_____

_____

_____

_____

List your Accelerators:

_____

_____

_____

_____

_____

_____

_____

List your Experts:

_____

_____

_____

_____

_____

_____

_____

_____

2. Markets

On the *Resource Map*, markets are any customer segments or industries that you have access to (e.g. financial services, healthcare, retail, social innovation space, etc)

_____

_____

_____

_____

_____

_____

_____

_____

3. Organizations

These are specific organizations that you have access to (it may be helpful to think about them in different sections such as non-profits, associations, for-profits, government agencies, etc)

_____

_____

_____

_____

_____

_____

_____

4. Capital

Sources of funding. This can include strategic partners, banks, angel investors, venture capital., etc.-- anywhere you can get more money or value for your personal or professional objective.

_____

_____

_____

_____

_____

_____

_____

5. Knowledge & Systems

Every individual or organization has some degree of knowledge or intellectual property at their disposal. Consider what you have in terms of intellectual property, systems, technology, etc.

_____

_____

_____

_____

_____

_____

_____

_____

6. Communications

What assets do you have in terms of communications? This can include websites, social media, human resources, public relations, marketing, etc.

_____

_____

_____

_____

_____

_____

_____

_____

Exercise 8: Create Your Year of Opportunity

Purpose

This exercise is intended to help you open your mind and begin thinking about the limitless opportunities around you. Don't censor yourself; let ideas flow and remain open to new possibilities even if they seem unlikely.

Instructions

Imagine that a year has passed and you have had the most extraordinary year you can imagine. You have created a _"Year of Opportunity."_

If you could design a _Year of Opportunity_ from your highest and best place, with absolutely no restrictions on what is possible, what would that year look like in your professional life? In your personal life? Imagine your perfect year.

_____

_____

_____

_____

_____

_____

_____

_____

_____

B. Now, with your *Year of Opportunity* in mind, what is the one goal or project that, if accomplished in the immediate future, would transform your business or your personal life?

_____

_____

_____

_____

_____

_____

_____

_____

C. What steps would you need to take to make this goal a reality?

_____

_____

_____

_____

_____

_____

_____

D. Would you need to purchase any special equipment, materials, or tools? Would you need any further education?

_____

_____

_____

_____

_____

_____

_____

E. What types of businesses/organizations/individuals would you need to employ?

_____

_____

_____

_____

_____

_____

_____

_____

F. Who do you know that could help you get in touch with those organizations/people?

_____

_____

_____

_____

_____

_____

_____

EXERCISE 9: Choosing an Opportunity

With your newly defined *SuccessDNA* from exercise 8 and your *Year of Opportunity* from exercise 9, consider what opportunities would be the best to break down into a real action plan.

1. Review your *Year of Opportunity* exercise. With your new knowledge of your *SuccessDNA*, what opportunity from that exercise do you want to create an action plan for? Why do you think it matches your *SuccessDNA*?

_____

_____

_____

_____

_____

_____

_____

_____

EXERCISE 10: Turn your vision into an Opportunity Plan

1. List the goals that you have for you or your organization based off of the opportunity you chose in exercise 10.

Make your goals tangible, but don't limit yourself to things like profits, sales, or growth- consider including personal satisfaction, environmental impact, product development, employee satisfaction, etc. The better de-fined your goals are, the easier it will be to achieve them.

_____

_____

_____

_____

_____

_____

_____

_____

2. Now list any objectives that come to mind when considering the most important goals from above. (Remember to consider the S.M.A.R.T. criteria outlined in Part 2 of this book.)

_____

_____

_____

_____

_____

_____

_____

_____

In Gratitude

In the spirit of the *Culture of Opportunity*, this book was co-created by a community of people, who all see the critical importance of business in the making of a more conscious, abundant, fairer and more sustainable world.

The First Leg

The first leg of my journey of bringing the *Culture of Opportunity* to the world came from being born at the intersection of business (my maternal grandparents- Joachim and Hannah Schultz, father's five brothers-George, Bill, Irving, Danny and Eddie Monchik and one sister, Lilian Polner) psychology (my father, Meyer Monchek was a psychiatrist and psychoanalyst far ahead of his time) my mother, Barbara Shilo, (an extraordinary painter and writer who created Silent Voices Speak the largest art exhibition on the Holocaust in history of San Francisco). And, my stepmother, Lisl Steiner, a groundbreaking photographer and oral historian and stepfather, Yacov Shilo, an innovator and entrepreneur in his own right.

The Second Leg

The second leg of the journey has come through the life lessons I have learned in collaborating with our clients and partners to build thriving, enduring companies. There are far too many to name here, but there are a few that stand out. Arthur Stein, Dick Jay, Deborah Kacprowicz, Joe Hermann and their team at Display Technologies taught me how unbridled passion and the willingness to leave the past behind can turn the "we never imagined we could do that" into "I don't think there is anything we can't achieve now." Gil Scharf, Keith Riehl , Steve Vigliotti, Brian Clark. Eileen McMahon and Roger Schwed, Ron Difrancesco of EuroBrokers/Maxcor and their unforgettable tribe who lost 62 members of their family on 9/11 taught me that no adversity is too great to turn into opportunity if there is unwavering commitment to a higher purpose. Mendel and Eugene Mendlowits, Barry Litwin, Yankel Zenwirth, Harry Drummer, Mel Reich, Lev Peker, Bill Parnes, Jerry Greenbaum, Rick Ungar and Howard Rhine of Adorama and their one of a kind team taught me that the patience and tenacity it takes to build and nurture a community of managers, associates and partners within an organization is well worth it. Mike Feltsman, Alex Vaysberg, Tye Atwood, Curtis Thompson, Sheri Coleman, Manuel Macchievelli, David Chase and their diverse team at Feltsberg taught me that careful and often precarious balancing act between risk and caution is essential for sustainable growth in our ever more turbulent world. Andy Gottesman, CEO of Edison Investment Advisors and Gottesman Realty Partners, taught me the power of both honoring and transcending family legacy. Scott Rechlar, Dave Gise, Eli Malinsky, Tonya Surman, Adil Dhalia, Chelsea Simpson, Dan Casey, Elizabeth Keane, Ron Livingston and all my friends at the Centre for Social Innovation, where the *Opportunity Lab* has called our home since 2013, have taught us the power of place and community in catalyzing social change through business. Thank you to Rich Berman Founder and CEO of Verb Factory, Lynn Rae Lowe founder of Metal Arts Gallery, Elyse Barbell and the team at the Literacy Assistance Center, Amita Nagaraja and the team at the Global Philanthropy Group at JP Morgan Chase for allowing us to grow through working with them. Of course, a special thank you to the entrepreneurs who granted us the opportunity to publish their case studies: Diana Ayton Shenker, CEO of Global Momenta, Carleton Nettleton and Ted Dikman, principals of Look Forward Consulting and their partner Jason Tanner and Colin Brice and Caleb Mulvena, Co-Founders of Mapos.

The Third Leg

The third leg of my journey came through a series of conversations with social entrepreneurs and conscious leaders beginning with Joy Anderson, Founder and CEO of Criterion Institute and Co-Founder of Good Capital, beginning in 2006. Joy, who introduced me to the world of social enterprise, encouraged me to publish the "Manifesto" of the *Opportunity Lab*, share it and allow it to have a life of its own. Then, Roger Frank of Innovare Advisors; Marissa Feinberg, founder of Green Spaces/Impact Hub-NYC and Triple Bottom Why; Kevin Jones and Rosemary Hardin co-founders of Mission Hub and SOCAP, Penelope Douglas, former Chairperson of Mission Hub; Tom Chi, Co-Founder of GoogleX, and with Ayesha Mathews Wadhwa, Co- Founders of Factory X; Dan Hendrix and Jim Hartzfeld, who helped to launch the Mission Zero sustainability initiative with the legendary Ray Anderson, founder of Interface; Scott Beck and Trish Groom of Tango; and Owen Hannay, CEO of Slingshot, Gabriel Brodbar and the NYU Reynolds community.

The Fourth Leg

The fourth and final leg has come through building and nurturing our team at the *Opportunity Lab*. Anna Staritsina, our Chief Empowerment Officer is our exemplar of excellence and commitment, Kate Lara, our Director of Operations and our book Project Manager, provides graceful wisdom to everything she does, Jaki Bradley, our Creative Director and book Co-Project Manager is a tireless advocate and innovator for our brand. Michael Stern, our book launch Project Manager provided exceptional care and attention to detail in getting the book out in the world. All have all played a central role in the development of the *Culture of Opportunity* methodology and its unique expression in the book. Mark Levy, my editor and mentor helped us see the potential of the book and honed its voice. Lynnea Brinkerhoff and Michael Pergola were invaluable thought partners in helping to shape the ideas in this book. Also, thanks to our Senior Advisors; Kevin Collins, Helene Rude and Bob Bellhouse.

Thank you to the people who helped us critique and bring the book into the world-our own *Opportunity Team*: Lisa Earle McLeod, Maryann Reid. David Shriner-Cahn, Gary Preston and Elaine Erickson, Noah Blumenthal, Greg Daugherty and John Natol, CEO of Pollen Brands who helped us see the power of design to tell our story. Tyler Wagner and his team at Authors Unite and Rachel Goldstein and the team at Agent of Change Tristan Thoma whose work was was essential in getting our book and its message out into the world.

In addition: special thanks to SOCAP/Mission Hub, Convergence, Wisdom 2.0, Shalom Mountain (Nance, Judi, Clara, Pamela, Kai and Jeff and the exceptional community of Shalom) The Journey (Brandon Bays, Kevin Billet, Skip and Kristine Lackey), Essence (Kabir and Ritama), Refocus and the other communities where I have learned and grown as a person. My family, dear friends and colleagues who have loved and supported me through the joys and pains of living: Ciara (my daughter who has taught me how to do difficult things with kindness and grace) and Jason Siegel, Pete and Karin Monchek (who set the bar for caring and commitment and unwavering support no matter the condition) Maia and Mason Monchek, Providencia Casado (who showed me how love and courage can overcome any adversity), Basilio Casado, Fred Rodriquez, Robert Le-Roy (a brilliant artist, second father to me and courageous partner with my mother), Robert Harrison and Robin Cooper, David Sadker and Karen Zittleman, Ed Poliandro and Phil Waldrop, Bob Stien and Enid Weishaus, Michael Blake, Sheila Blackmond, Myriam Laureano and Marggie Melendez, Rose and Jay Agar, Steve Muchnick, Marc and Linda Press, Bobbi Van (who helped me see what was possible in my life and work), Leslie Grossman, Marc Halpert and many more.

Notes

Anderson, R. C. (2009). Confessions of a Radical Industrialist . St. Martin's Press.

Jeszeck, C. A. (2015). Contingent Workforce: Size, Characteristics, Earnings, and Benefits. Washington, D.C.: U.S. Government Accountability Office.

Labor Force Statistics from the Current Population Survey. (2016, February 10). Retrieved January 15, 2017, from Bureau of Labor Statistics: https://www.bls.gov/cps/cpsaat36.htm

Mishel, L. (2013, January 30). Economic Policy Institute. Retrieved January 15, 2017, from Vast majority of wage earners are working harder, and for not much more: http://www.epi.org/publication/ib348-trends-us-work-hours-wages-1979-2007/

Morelix, A., Fairlie, R. W., Russell, J., Reedy, E., & Tareque, I. (2016). Retrieved January 15, 2017, from The Kauffman Index of Main Street Entrepreneurship: National Trends: http://www.kauffman.org/~/media/kauffman_org/microsites/kauffman_index/main_street_2016/kauffman_index_main_street_national_trends_2016.pdf

Reich, R. B. (2015). Saving Capitalism: For the Many, Not the Few. New York: Alfred A. Knopf.

About Mark Monchek

After decades of growing entrepreneurial businesses and nonprofits, Mark's mission is to live with passion, grace and joy, creating shared opportunity with the people he loves and the causes he believes in.

As Founder and Chief Opportunity Officer of the *Opportunity Lab*, he works to empower conscious leaders to build great organizations that make a positive difference in the world. Mark leverages his expertise in public speaking, writing and consulting to create programs that spark innovation and growth. He is a passionate storyteller and facilitator of meaningful dialogue, and his ultimate goal is to build a community of like-minded conscious business and nonprofit leaders committed to Doing Well by Doing Good.

He has worked with leaders from JP Morgan Chase, Google, Apple, Etsy, General Electric, Goldman Sachs, The New York Times, Wharton, Edison Properties, NBC, Paxar, Time Warner, United Nations, United Way of Greater New York, and Adorama to help them take their organizations to the next level of sustainable growth.

Mark is a graduate of New York University and the Greenwich Institute for Psychoanalytic Studies and has served as adjunct faculty for Columbia University, New York University and the College of New Rochelle. He is an author, public speaker and mentor. He has directed and produced two short films and was lead interviewer and creative consultant on Politics Con Sabor-The History of Latino Politics in New York State. His work has also been featured on the WCBS, Lifetime, Smashing the Plateau, Champions of Social Good, The OD Network Press, That Matters, Conscious Talk Radio, Catalyst, Newsday, Working Women Magazine, and The San Francisco Chronicle.

The best way to predict the future is to invent it."

Alan Kay, Computer Scientist, Professor and Jazz Musician

About the Opportunity Lab

The *Opportunity Lab* is a strategy and leadership development and consulting firm that empowers leaders to sustainably grow their organizations and make a positive difference in the world. We help leaders and their teams discover, evaluate, and launch the right opportunities to keep them growing in any economy, create jobs that spark the passion of their people, and experiences that are better for customers, communities and the environment-- all by leveraging the resources they already have.

We do this in three ways: we partner with clients to co-create lasting systems for growth and strategy, we train high-performing teams and individuals through our transformational programs and workshops, and we help support tomorrow's leaders and managers through personalized coaching, retreats, and speaking engagements.

To learn more about The *Opportunity Lab*, please contact us at:

The Centre for Social Innovation
601 West 26th St Suite 325-15
New York NY 10001

212-367-2054

www.opplab.com

discover@opplab.com